THIS BOOK IS ABOUT **YOU**

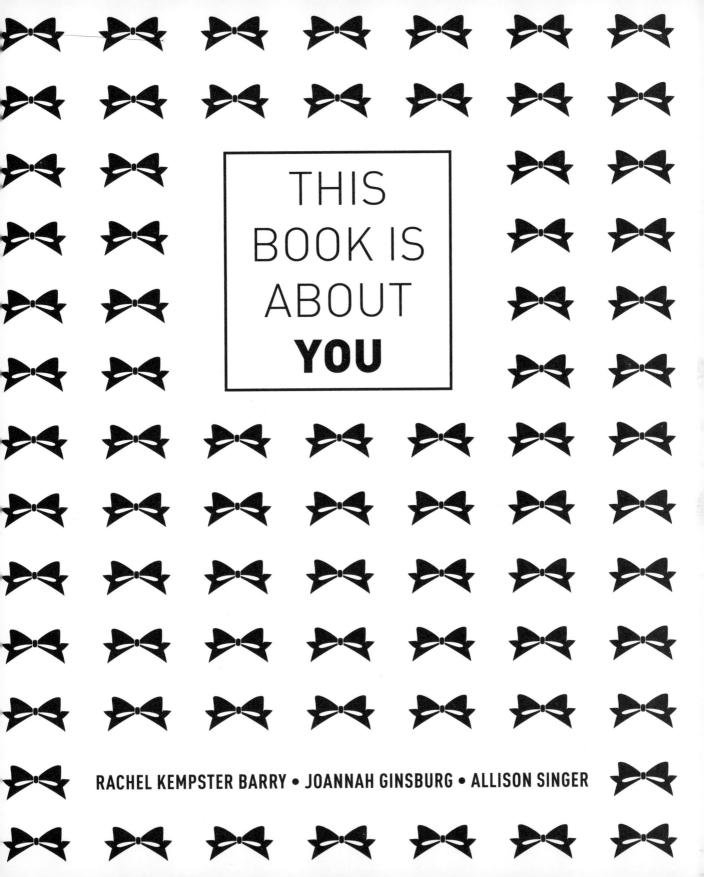

THIS
BOOK IS
ABOUT
YOU

RACHEL KEMPSTER BARRY • JOANNAH GINSBURG • ALLISON SINGER

Senior Designer Jessica Lee
Editorial Director Nancy Ellwood
Senior Editor Margaret Parrish
Producer, Pre-production David Almond
Senior Producer Gary Batchelor

First American Edition, 2017
Published in the United States by DK Publishing
345 Hudson Street, New York, NY 10014

Copyright © 2017 Dorling Kindersley Limited
DK, a Division of Penguin Random House LLC
17 18 19 20 21 10 9 8 7 6 5 4 3 2 1
001–298447–Jul/2017

All rights reserved.
Without limiting the rights under the copyright
reserved above, no part of this publication may be
reproduced, stored in or introduced into a retrieval
system, or transmitted, in any form, or by any means
(electronic, mechanical, photocopying, recording, or
otherwise), without the prior written permission of
the copyright owner.
Published in Great Britain by Dorling Kindersley
Limited.

A catalog record for this book is available from the
Library of Congress.
ISBN 978-1-4654-5657-1

DK books are available at special discounts when
purchased in bulk for sales promotions, premiums,
fund-raising, or educational use.
For details, contact: DK Publishing Special Markets,
345 Hudson Street, New York, NY 10014
SpecialSales@dk.com

Printed and bound in China

All images © Dorling Kindersley Limited
For further information see: www.dkimages.com

A WORLD OF IDEAS:
SEE ALL THERE IS TO KNOW

www.dk.com

CONTENTS

Books have been
written about lots of important
people—kings and queens, masters of
business, famous thinkers and doers and makers,
American presidents, Justin Bieber . . . . But this book,
this one that you have here in your hands, was written
about someone *extremely* important:

YOU!

At least, it will be, once you've finished it. We three authors will take you
as far as we can. After that, we'll need your help. Between these covers,
you'll find all sorts of quizzes, questionnaires, activities, and thought
experiments, all designed to help you figure out your . . .

PAST: Who were you then, and how have you changed? What about
your past still impacts your life now? What choices did you make
that led you to where you are now? Look back, and gain the
information and understanding you need to forge ahead.

PRESENT: Take a break from your daily routine, and look
around. What and who and where are you today?
The people you hang with, the activities you do,
the thoughts you have—what do they say
about who you are as a person?

FUTURE: Where are you going tomorrow? A year from now? A decade from now? What are your goals, your plans, your dreams? Sharpen what you see when you look ahead, and you'll see how bright your future really is.

Look, we're not experts on your life. (Well, one of us is—you're in good hands with Joannah, who's literally an expert on teen psychology.) Only you know the answers to the questions in these pages.

And you should totally make this book yours. Go through it from front to back, or back to front, or skip to the sections that seem the most interesting. Do the activities solo, or grab a friend to help you. Read the book upside down, if that's one of your talents. Too many interactive journals are filled with quizzes that have one "right" answer. That's not how we roll. We want you to make this book *your* book, exactly the way you want it to be, whatever that looks like.

Because don't forget: This book is about YOU. Your past, your present, your future. Your amazing, wonderful, confusing, complicated life.

RACHEL, JOANNAH, AND ALLIE

-*This*-
CHAPTER
IS ABOUT YOUR
PAST

"YOUR PAST IS ALWAYS YOUR PAST.
EVEN IF YOU FORGET IT,
IT REMEMBERS YOU."

–SARAH DESSEN, *WHAT HAPPENED TO GOODBYE*

"... growing up happens
when you start having
things you look back on and
wish you could change."

—CASSANDRA CLARE, *CITY OF ASHES*

What Do You
Remember?

Hey, remember that time you were a baby, chilling out in your crib, goo-goo-ing and ga-ga-ing and sucking on a pacifier? No? Yeah, we didn't think so. (If you do remember, you're pretty amazing—experts have found that very few people can remember anything that happened to them before the age of three.)

Because we only have so much room in our long-term memories, often the nonessential stuff gets thrown out to make room for what's really important. So it's fair to assume the memories that you've kept on your brain-shelf the longest are there for a reason.

Think back, as far back as you can. What are your earliest memories? And why do you think they've stuck around?

When I was ___ years old, I remember:

....
....
....

Why this memory is important to me:

....
....
....

When I was ___ years old, I remember:

....
....
....

Why this memory is important to me:

....
....
....

When I was ___ years old, I remember:

....
....
....

Why this memory is important to me:

....
....
....

When I was ___ years old, I remember:

....
....
....

Why this memory is important to me:

....
....
....

When I was ___ years old, I remember:

....
....
....

Why this memory is important to me:

....
....
....

When I was ___ years old, I remember:

....
....
....

Why this memory is important to me:

....
....
....

What Do You **Remember?**

CONTINUED

Memory lets us store and retrieve information about the world. There are many things you can do to improve your memory—including putting it to the test.

These activities test your short-term memory; that's what you hold in your mind from what you've just heard, read, or seen. In these exercises, your goal is to look at the material once, try to retain it, and then recall it as best you can. Ready for a memory workout?

1: **What's your limit?**

Below are a few rows of numbers. Starting with the shortest row, read the numbers once and then cover the row. Can you recall the numbers in the order you read them?

```
5 7 0 4 8 2 6 3 1 9
8 2 5 3 0 7 1 6 4
2 9 4 0 7 1 3 8
4 7 1 3 8 6 2
8 4 6 2 5 9
4 9 0 3 1
5 2 1 8
```

Your digit span = how many numbers you recalled correctly before you got your first row wrong.

>> Your Score (your digit span):

_____

(from 4 to 10)

2: **Chair colors**

On the phone, the furniture salesperson tells you the six available colors for the armchair you want to buy for your room. You need to remember the names of these colors until you can write them down.

Read the names of these six colors once. Then cover them while repeating the six names to yourself for 10 seconds. Can you write them in the space below?

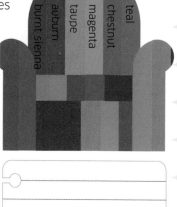

teal
chestnut
magenta
taupe
auburn
burnt sienna

>> How many did you remember?

3: Cluster of shapes

Study this picture of overlapping shapes for 5 seconds. Then cover it and reproduce what you remember in the space provided.

>> **Were you close?**
(This is a tricky one)

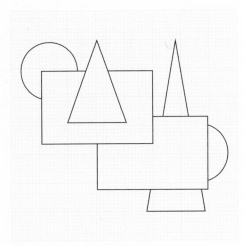

4: Cat invasion!

The seven cats on the top wall have invaded your backyard. Look at them once, then cover them and study the cats on the bottom wall. Very quickly, circle the cats that have *never* been in your backyard.

>> **How many did you spot correctly?**

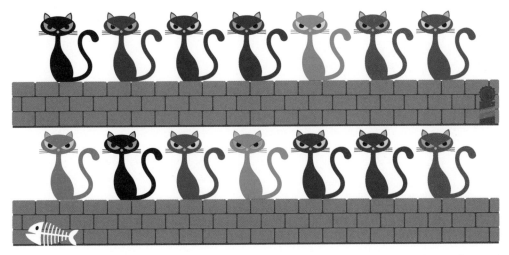

15

Your family

Families are like snowflakes—no two are the same. Answer the questions below to find out if your family is Kardashian-esque, classic all-American fun, or somewhere in between.

1 **Your family's idea of a perfect vacation is:**

A. a pizza tour of NYC
B. Paris in the spring
C. camping in the Rockies
D. exploring art museums and monuments
E. fun-packed beaches and water parks

2 **Your go-to family restaurant spot is:**

A. a local gastropub with killer *frites*
B. anywhere that the people-watching is better than the food
C. the nearest vegetarian or vegan cafe
D. your kitchen table—you rarely go out for dinner
E. a kitschy hot dog stand that serves amazing milk shakes

3 **It's movie night! What do you choose to watch together?**

A. Any *Harry Potter* movie (or all of them!)
B. *Titanic*
C. *Babe*
D. a documentary about global warming
E. *The Princess Bride*

4 **What song gets your whole family out on the dance floor?**

A. The *Star Wars* theme song
B. "Vogue"
C. "So Happy Together"
D. Jazz—any sort of jazz
E. "Shut Up and Dance"

5 If your family were an article of clothing, what would it be?

A. Converse sneakers

B. a fur vest

C. Birkenstocks

D. pleated pants

E. a rainbow wig

6 If your family were a car, it would be:

A. the Batmobile

B. an Aston Martin

C. a vintage Volkswagen van

D. a Volvo

E. an ice-cream truck

7 You're making dessert for your parents' anniversary. You choose:

A. a *Doctor Who* cake shaped like a Tardis

B. Baked Alaska

C. an enormous fruit salad

D. lemon bars

E. brownie sundaes

8 Uh-oh! You got a C in Science. How do your parents react?

A. "It's just one grade. You'll do better next time."

B. "We're sending you to military school tonight!"

C. "It's because you refused to dissect the frog, isn't it?"

D. "We're sending you to military school . . . eventually."

E. "You can't win them all. Who wants ice cream?"

9 There's a flood in the basement! What does your family do?

A. invites the neighbors over, orders pizza, and has a mopping party

B. posts pictures to Instagram and Facebook

C. makes sure the basement spiders don't drown

D. calls the insurance company

E. goes for a swim

10 Your family's spirit animal is:

A. a bunny named Roger Rabbit

B. a Capuchin monkey

C. a turtle from a rescue shelter

D. a hairless cat

E. a big, slobbery dog

Your family

IF YOU ANSWERED MOSTLY As:
You have a nerdy, fun family!
The family that cosplays together, stays together. Your family knows how to have a good time making robots, comic-book shopping, or waiting in line to be the first to see the latest superhero movie.

IF YOU ANSWERED MOSTLY Bs:
Your family has a flair for drama.
If a camera crew followed your family around, they could turn the footage into a hit TV show. Life in your world is always a little bit crazy, a little bit glam, and a little bit fancy—and you wouldn't have it any other way.

IF YOU ANSWERED MOSTLY Cs: Your family is as organic as they come.
Your dad had everyone eating kale and quinoa before they were hot new trends. You have fond memories of planting the family garden, working with your neighbors on volunteer projects, and hiking every trail in a 100-mile radius. Chances are slim you've ever had a fried Oreo, and that's OK.

IF YOU ANSWERED MOSTLY Ds:
Your family is serious.
You work hard, your parents work hard, and you play hard, too. Your family kayaking trip might turn more competitive than the Olympics, but that spirit helps push you to be the best you can be. Sometimes you want to let loose, and that's cool—just make sure you get your homework finished first.

IF YOU ANSWERED MOSTLY Es: Your family is fun-loving and a little nuts.
Your yard is always the most crazily decorated for Halloween, and your mom sometimes sends you to school with an all-candy lunch (Swedish Fish are kind of like tuna, right?). Sometimes all the fun makes you a little crazy, but you can't imagine growing up with a family any less eccentric.

"The family—that dear octopus from whose tentacles we never quite escape, nor in our innermost hearts ever quite wish to." **–DODIE SMITH**

YOUR CHILDHOOD FAVORITES

For little kids, "favorites" take over their whole lives. If your favorite color was purple, for instance, purple was probably everywhere: painted on your walls and in every outfit you wore. The purple crayons in your crayon box were very likely worn down to stubs. If your parents had let you dye your hair, you can guess which color it would have been.

Think back, way back, waaaaay back, into the distant past, back to when you were five. (OK, that isn't actually so long ago.) What were your favorites then? And are they same now?

Your favorite **color** was:

Now it's:

Your favorite **song** was:

Now it's:

Your favorite **animal** was:

Now it's:

Your favorite **TV show** was:

Now it's:

Your favorite **movie** was:

Now it's:

Your favorite **friend** was:

Now it's:

Your favorite **activity** was:

Now it's:

Your favorite **book** was:

Now it's:

Your favorite **outfit** was:

Now it's:

Your favorite **meal** was:

Now it's:

Your favorite **snack** was:

Now it's:

Your favorite **sport** was:

Now it's:

Your favorite **number** was:

Now it's:

SHARE YOUR STORY

Before books were widely available, most people told stories to remember the past and to share it with future generations. Stories were entertainment in a time before Netflix. Medieval troubadours shared stories old and new. The fictional Scheherazade used stories to save herself from execution—she told 1,000 stories so enchanting that the king spared her life day after day so he could hear more of her tales.

Stories are powerful, and you already have many to tell.

Use the next page to tell a story from your own personal history. Maybe it's a tale of daring (the time you scaled a tree to rescue the neighbor's kitten). Maybe it's a tale of woe (the time you visited your grandma in the hospital). Include the sorts of details that will draw in your audience: Make them feel the scrubby tree branches flick across your ankles as you make your way to the kitten. Explain the soft hospital sounds you heard while holding your grandma's hand, the whoosh of the machines, the footsteps of the nurses.

After you've written your story, read it out loud. Read it aloud again and again until you've memorized it, or most of it. Practice reading it in front of a mirror to see how your face changes from beginning to end.

If you're feeling brave, tell your story to a friend. If you're feeling very brave, share it at the school talent show, or an open mic night at a local coffee shop or bookstore.

START YOUR STORY HERE:

THE FIRST TIME YOU...

If something traumatic happened the first time you went somewhere, you'd probably be in NO hurry to go there again. If you felt amazing the first time you tried a new activity, you'd likely jump right back in. First impressions last a lifetime—it's true of people, and it's true of experiences.

What are some first times that stand out as being important, for good or for bad? After you've filled in this page, consider: Has your impression of that particular thing, person, or experience changed? Did your first experience define your lifelong opinion, or have you let it grow since then?

The **FIRST TIME** I
had a sleepover with
a friend
was *two years* ago
and I remember feeling
*happy, excited, and a
little nervous.*

The **FIRST TIME** I

was ago
and I remember feeling

The **FIRST TIME** I

was ago
and I remember feeling

The **FIRST TIME** I

was ago
and I remember feeling

The **FIRST TIME** I

was ago
and I remember feeling

The **FIRST TIME** I

was ago
and I remember feeling

The **FIRST TIME** I

was ago
and I remember feeling

HOW DO YOU
shine?

You've thought about the people, places, and experiences that have affected your life. Now let's check in with how you've affected theirs. On the next page, you'll be making a sunshine map. Write your name at the center, and on each ray of sunshine, write the name of someone or something you've affected in a positive way. It can be:

a person (a friend, a sibling, a teacher, a baby-sitting charge . . .)
a group (a sports team, your youth group, your band, your classmates . . .)
a place (your school, your home, your favorite bookstore, a nearby park . . .)

If you can think of something else you've affected positively (like a special cause or charity), go ahead and add it. This is *your* map.

When you've filled in all of the rays, decorate the page however you like. Your personal sunshine map is there to remind you just how special and important you are to the world around you. You shine!

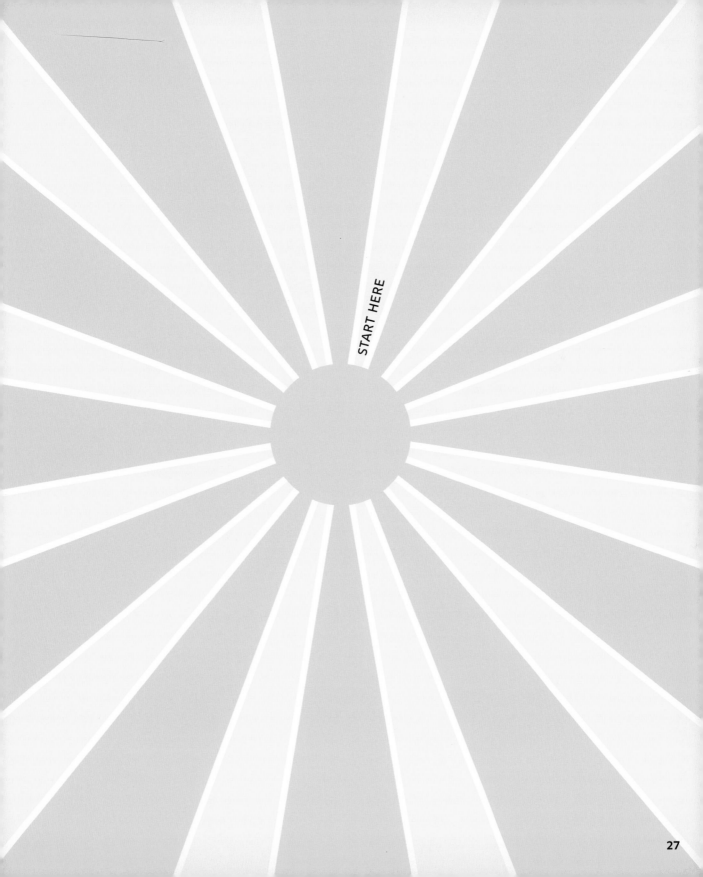

START HERE

WHO
WOULD YOU CALL?

There are people you talk to every day because they're in your world every day—your parents, your teachers, your friends at school. Maybe you have a best friend who you talk to or text every day, too. But now we're asking you to think a little deeper about the people you know and talk to most.

Maybe your mom is a great listener, but you're worried she'll share what you tell her on Facebook. Maybe you can tell your best friend anything, but sometimes you'd like to keep a few secrets to yourself. How do the people in your support system rate as listeners, advice givers, and cheerleaders?

Answer the questions on the next page as honestly as you can, and really think about your answers. Coming up with answers might not be that easy.

You entered an Instagram contest to meet your favorite band. And you won!
Who you do tell first? Why?

....
....
....
....
....
....
....

Your mom got a fantastic new job, but it means your family needs to move to London for at least two years.
Who do you tell first? Why?

....
....
....
....
....
....

After studying really, really hard for a month you still eke out only a C on your final exam. You're so disappointed you had to hold back tears in class.
Who do you tell first? Why?

....
....
....
....
....
....

Your best friend suddenly stops talking to you. Monday, everything's fine. Tuesday, she never shows up at your lunch table. You text, she won't text back. It's all just totally bizarre.
Who do you tell first? Why?

....
....
....
....
....

You have an absolutely perfect day. Everything went right.
Who do you tell first? Why?

....
....
....
....
....
....
....

You have an absolutely terrible day. Everything went wrong.
Who do you tell first? Why?

....
....
....
....
....
....

WHAT DID YOU
Believe?

Here are a couple of
things we had to unlearn:
Hermione is not pronounced
HER-ME-OH-KNEE.
If you eat a watermelon seed,
a watermelon will not grow in
your stomach.

True Story: A friend of ours was cleaning out her mess of a closet. Her first task was to take everything out and make orderly piles. As she neared the end of the first giant pile of T-shirts, she found a silver cup. Curious. It was engraved with her name and a mysterious date—May 5, 2000. That wasn't her birthday—she was born in April. She was afraid her heart was going to beat right out of her chest, because she knew this could mean one thing, and one thing only: She was adopted. Her parents kept it a secret. That had to be it. For a week she simmered with sadness and anger, never feeling brave or strong enough to confront her parents. One night her mom called her in for dinner, and she brought the cup and held it out boldly toward her mom.

"You found your Christening cup!" her mom said.

"Um, Christening cup? What's that?" she said.

"You had a Christening when you were a baby. It's tradition to get a cup engraved with that date. Why? What did you think it was?"

"Nothing, Mom. Didn't have a clue."

We all have moments in life where we imagine something to be true and it turns out we were dead wrong. Sometimes it's a version of history we're told in school (Wait—Columbus coming to America wasn't all sunshine and roses?). Or something we're told by our parents. True or False: A fairy leaves money under your pillow when you lose your teeth.

Use this page to record all the things you've misunderstood. Don't forget to save some room for the things you'll someday learn you got wrong.

DATE:

What I Thought Was True: ....

....

....

What's the Real Truth: ....

....

....

Why I Was wrong: ....

....

....

DATE:

What I Thought Was True: ....

....

....

What's the Real Truth: ....

....

....

Why I Was Wrong: ....

....

....

DATE:

What I Thought Was True: ....

....

....

What's the Real Truth: ....

....

....

Why I Was Wrong: ....

....

....

DATE:

What I Thought Was True: ....

....

....

What's the Real Truth: ....

....

....

Why I Was Wrong: ....

....

....

DATE:

What I Thought Was True: ....

....

....

What's the Real Truth: ....

....

....

Why I Was Wrong: ....

....

....

DATE:

What I Thought Was True: ....

....

....

What's the Real Truth: ....

....

....

Why I Was Wrong: ....

....

....

Are You **Embarrassed?**

Have you ever said, "If only I had done this, instead of that"? Ugh. We all have. Embarrassing situations are part of life, and we all make decisions we wish we hadn't. The reality is, we make what we *think* is the best decision with the information we have at the time. What is most important is how you handle an embarrassing situation.

How would you most likely handle the following potentially embarrassing scenarios?

SCENARIO 1

FACEBOOK STALKER

Last night, trying to look up the cute new boy at school, you accidentally posted his name as your status instead of searching for him. Your reaction is to:

A. Quickly follow up with a new status post, tag him in it, and laugh it off: "Well, if THAT wasn't everyone's worst nightmare. I guess there are no secrets here!"

B. Get really mad at yourself, then immediately decide that you are coming down with the flu and will have to miss the next week of school.

C. Feel a little silly, but realize it's not that big a deal. At least Eric knows who you are now! No one will be talking about this by next week anyway.

SCENARIO 2

SPOIL ME

Your parents lost their jobs and had to cut your allowance. When a classmate asks why you haven't gotten the new iPhone or been going out as much lately, you:

A. Reply honestly. You know deep down that the things you own don't define the person you are, and that tense times come and go.

B. Complain about how unfair it is that you can't go out and get the things you want. You get mad that your parents are such a mess.

C. You try to blow it off and change the subject, but deep down you can't help feeling embarrassed by your family's financial problems.

SCENARIO 3

SOCCER SNOB

After leaving the team you played with for years for a more competitive one, you find that you don't like your new teammates or coach. Worse, your former teammates think you're a snob for leaving. You:

A. Tell your old teammates that you just wanted to push yourself out of your comfort zone, and talk to your new team and coach about how you can fit in better.

B. Feel sorry for yourself. You messed up a good thing and should have just left well enough alone. You consider quitting soccer altogether.

C. Ignore your old teammates, and although you're a little crabby every time you have to go to practice with your new team, you resolve to make the best of your decision.

SCENARIO 4

PICTURE THIS

A girl you used to be friends with is showing a very unflattering picture of you to your classmates. She knows it embarrasses you, but doesn't stop. You react by:

A. Understanding that everyone has bad pictures and ignoring it. But if you think the girl is showing that picture to try to make you feel bad, you'll confront her about being a bully.

B. Feeling horrible about yourself. You are going to set your alarm 40 minutes earlier from now on so you can spend more time looking photo-ready!

C. Knowing that some days we feel cuter than others, and it's not outside appearances that are most important, but who we are on the inside that counts. You decide not to let that photo bother you.

Quiz Analysis

If you have mostly A answers:
You're usually comfortable tackling situations head-on and being straightforward about addressing what has happened. You can see both sides and recognize that most situations are not all good or all bad. You tend to be diplomatic and mature in your responses.

MOSTLY

MOSTLY

If you have mostly B answers:
These are very understandable reactions. Many times we just want to disappear in the face of embarrassment. You are entitled to hide in your cocoon for a while and let the storm pass; just make sure you aren't too hard on yourself. When you reemerge, try not to dwell!

MOSTLY

If you have mostly C answers:
You are a grin-and-bear-it kind of person, and you tend to focus on what's next. You are honest with yourself about when something hasn't gone perfectly, but you don't get too caught up in negative situations or circumstances.

THE FOLLOWING TOOLS AND EXERCISES ARE HELPFUL FOR DEALING WITH EMBARRASSING SITUATIONS AND REGRETS. WHICH WORKS BEST FOR YOU?

STAYING POSITIVE

Don't let embarrassments or regrets become a part of you. It's easy to let negative feelings affect your confidence or self-worth. Forgive yourself for your mistakes.

HUMOR

Humor is a great way to deflect embarrassment. It lets you address the situation while keeping things light.

EDUCATION

In any situation, embarrassing or otherwise, there are always things to be learned. What can this regret or embarrassing situation teach you?

COMMUNICATION

Sometimes the most obvious things to say are the hardest things to say! Don't get caught up with what you *think* you should say, or what you *think* might sound best. Be honest about your feelings.

THINK ABOUT IT: DO YOU HAVE ANY REGRETS? WHAT ARE THEY? WHY DO YOU THINK YOU MADE THOSE DECISIONS? WOULD YOU BE ABLE TO MAKE BETTER DECISIONS NOW THAN YOU DID THEN?

My, How You've Changed

Have you ever looked back and thought to yourself how different you are now from how you used to be? It can be empowering to realize how far you've come, and how you've grown and changed. One of the most exciting things about getting older is your ever-evolving ability to make things happen. When something isn't working, you have the power to figure out a new approach. In what ways have you changed since you were a kid?

For each of the following situations, first write how you would have handled it when you were younger. Then write how you would handle the situation now.

Getting along with friends or siblings

Managing disappointment

Showing off victories

Feeling like life is unfair

Feeling misunderstood or like no one cares

Talking to your parents

Working toward your goals

THINK ABOUT IT: For which situations did your reactions change the most? Why do you think your reactions to these situations changed so much?

WHAT'S YOUR **LIE?**

Here's how to share stories from your past with a friend in a super-fun way. On this page, write down six facts about yourself, and one falsehood. On the next page, have your friend do the same. Switch pages with your friend, and each of you try to guess the other's lie.

01

02

03

04

05

06

07

For example, if Emma Watson were filling out this page, she'd say:

✔ 1. I was born in Paris.
✔ 2. I starred in my first Harry Potter film when I was just 11.
✔ 3. I'm a certified yoga teacher.
✘ 4. My parents are famous British stage actors.
✔ 5. I have a bachelor's degree in English Literature from
     Brown University.
✔ 6. I'm proud to be a UN Goodwill Ambassador.
✔ 7. I love cats.

(It's #4 that's false—her parents are both lawyers!)

01

02

03

04

05

06

07

YOUR OWN WOMEN ROCK! CALENDAR

JANUARY

6 Joan of Arc is born (c.1412)

FEBRUARY

15 Susan B. Anthony's birthday (1820)

MARCH

Women's History Month

APRIL

2 Jeannette Rankin of Montana is formally seated in the US House of Representatives as the first woman elected to Congress (1917)

MAY

29 "Rosie the Riveter" by Norman Rockwell appears on the cover of *The Saturday Evening Post* (1943)

JUNE

18 Sally Ride becomes the first American woman in space (1983)

In March we celebrate Women's History Month—a time to honor the amazing achievements of women across time and across the world. From the groundbreaking science of Marie Curie to the athletic achievements of Venus and Serena Williams, we honor the risk-takers and the brave spirits who paved the way for equality.

But why celebrate only one month a year? Celebrate the amazing achievements of women (from your mom to Malala) all the time with our WOMEN ROCK! calendar. We've filled in a few names to get you started, but the rest is up to you. Celebrate your awesome aunt in August (her favorite month), or an inspiring author's birthday. With a little Googling, you'll have a calendar chock-full of milestones, anniversaries, and other great dates worth celebrating year-round.

JULY

12 Malala Yousafzai's Birthday (1997)

AUGUST

18 The 19th Amendment to the United States Constitution granted American women the right to vote (1920)

SEPTEMBER

25 Sandra Day O'Connor is sworn in as the first woman US Supreme Court Justice (1981)

OCTOBER

8 Toni Morrison becomes the first African American woman to win the Nobel Prize for Literature (1993)

NOVEMBER

18 Wilma Mankiller's birthday (1945). Mankiller was the first female Chief of the Cherokee Nation

DECEMBER

1 Rosa Parks sparks the US Civil Rights Movement by refusing to give up her seat on a bus to a white person (1955)

THE **HISTORY** AROUND YOU

There are family stories you probably hear a lot. The time your mom locked the keys in the car along with your baby brother. Or the story of how your grandpa got the nickname Mousey because his voice sounded really squeaky when he was a kid.

On this page write down the family stories you know by heart. Depending on the size of your family, you might need to paste in some extra pages (feel free)!

You may not have heard some family stories before. Ask someone in your family—your mom, your grandpa, your aunt who lives in France—to tell you a story they've never told you. If they need some prompting, you might ask:

• Were you ever in the newspaper for doing something cool?
• Did you ever help someone out of a difficult situation?
• Who was your best friend when you were 15?
• What's the happiest day you ever had?

Ask them if it's OK for you to write their stories down in your book. If not, that's OK, too! It's still cool that you know something new about someone you love.

Check Your Programming

Guess what? You're a robot.

OK, not really. But just like robots are programmed to respond to commands and perform specifics tasks, your past has programmed you to react and think in certain ways in certain situations. This isn't a bad thing. When you put your hand on something scalding hot, for example, your programming tells you to get your hand off it before you get burned. Or if you're in a place where you don't feel comfortable, your programming kicks in to get you out of there.

But when our programmed responses aren't what we'd like them to be, we have reprogramming to do. Were you programmed to be polite and let others speak first, but that's hurting you in class because your thoughts don't get heard? Were you programmed always to speak your mind, but now you're hurting people's feelings with your extreme honesty? Do you spend too much time refreshing a website or watching a TV show you don't care about, just out of habit? Time to do some debugging (that's programmer-speak for "problem solving").

HERE'S HOW TO DO IT:

>> 1. PAY ATTENTION:
Pay attention to yourself and your reactions and impulses during the day. Is there anything you're doing that doesn't feel right?

>> 2. ASSESS:
Is that the way you wish you'd have acted in, or reacted to, a certain situation? If not, what do you wish you had done? Why?

>> 3. PLAN:
What are you going to do the next time this situation comes up? Speak up? Consider other people's feelings? Change the channel?

>> 4. MAKE IT HAPPEN:
Put your plan into action. It can be hard to go against your instincts, but once you've decided to make a change, there's only one thing to do—make it happen!

Turn the page for more info

Check Your Programming

WHAT DO YOU WANT TO CHANGE?

WHY DO YOU WANT TO CHANGE IT?

HOW ARE YOU GOING TO CHANGE IT?

AFTER YOU PUT YOUR PLAN INTO ACTION,
WHAT WERE THE RESULTS?

WHAT DO YOU WANT TO CHANGE?

WHY DO YOU WANT TO CHANGE IT?

HOW ARE YOU GOING TO CHANGE IT?

AFTER YOU PUT YOUR PLAN INTO ACTION,
WHAT WERE THE RESULTS?

WHAT DO YOU WANT TO CHANGE?

HOW ARE YOU GOING TO CHANGE IT?

WHY DO YOU WANT TO CHANGE IT?

AFTER YOU PUT YOUR PLAN INTO ACTION, WHAT WERE THE RESULTS?

WHAT DO YOU WANT TO CHANGE?

HOW ARE YOU GOING TO CHANGE IT?

WHY DO YOU WANT TO CHANGE IT?

AFTER YOU PUT YOUR PLAN INTO ACTION, WHAT WERE THE RESULTS?

Ta-da!
YOU'RE AN
Artist

When a preschooler draws a picture, you better believe they're proud of themselves. The fact that their (usually unidentifiable) creation isn't going to be winning any awards doesn't mean anything to them. It's the fact that they made something, something they love, with colors and crayons and stickers and whatever-the-heck-else they love. When was the last time you made a piece of art like that?

Here's your chance. Let these two pages be your blank canvas, and draw (or paint, or sticker, or collage, or . . .) whatever your inner child wants. Don't think—just create!

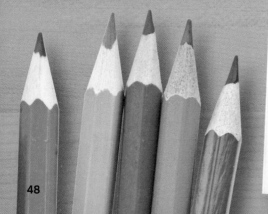

GO WITH YOUR GUT:

TIRED OF ALL THE THINKING THIS BOOK IS MAKING YOU DO? IT'S TIME TO GO WITH YOUR GUT. CIRCLE YOUR ANSWERS BELOW. **WOULD YOU RATHER** . . .

REMEMBER ABSOLUTELY **EVERYTHING**

OR

REMEMBER ABSOLUTELY **NOTHING?**

CARRY YOUR FAVORITE CHILDHOOD DOLL OR STUFFED ANIMAL WITH YOU **TO SCHOOL**

OR

MISPLACE IT?

STAY EXACTLY THE SAME AS YOU ARE NOW

OR

CHANGE WHO YOU ARE COMPLETELY?

HOLD TIGHT TO YOUR BELIEFS

OR

BE OPEN TO CHANGING WHAT YOU BELIEVE?

HAVE **LOTS OF LITTLE** EMBARRASSING MOMENTS

OR

HAVE **ONE MAJORLY** EMBARRASSING MOMENT?

HAVE A VERY **BIG** FAMILY

OR

HAVE A VERY **SMALL** FAMILY?

LOOK AT OLD **FAMILY PHOTOS**

OR

WATCH OLD **FAMILY VIDEOS?**

PAST

BE ABLE TO TELL WHEN SOMEONE IS LYING — **OR** — **BE ABLE TO LIE** WITHOUT ANYONE NOTICING?

MEET **GEORGE WASHINGTON** — **OR** — MEET **ABRAHAM LINCOLN**?

MEET **JANIS JOPLIN** — **OR** — MEET **MARILYN MONROE**?

STAR ON YOUR FAVORITE CHILDHOOD **TV SHOW** — **OR** — STAR IN YOUR FAVORITE CHILDHOOD **MOVIE**?

HAVE GROWN UP IN **ONE PLACE** — **OR** — HAVE LIVED IN **MANY DIFFERENT PLACES**?

TRAVEL IN A TIME MACHINE **TO THE PAST** — **OR** — TRAVEL IN A TIME MACHINE **TO THE FUTURE**?

HAVE BEEN A **FAMOUS CHILD** ACTOR — **OR** — HAD A **NORMAL** CHILDHOOD?

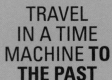

GO BACK IN TIME TO **WHEN YOU WERE FIVE** — **OR** — GO BACK IN TIME TO **YESTERDAY**?

CHANGE THE THING IN YOUR PAST YOU MOST **REGRET** — **OR** — LEARN FROM IT AND **MOVE ON**?

HOW DID YOU GET HERE?

No one becomes the world's greatest baker without ever having made a perfect soufflé (and countless failed ones). No one becomes a famous athlete without ever having won a game (or lost a lot of them). If you have the best grades in class, you've probably had to study hard. Everyone's journey is different, but everyone has a journey. Let's look at yours.

In this exercise, you'll retrace the steps that got you to where you are today. And that's important—because knowing how you got to this point is the first step in figuring out how to get to the next step in your life.

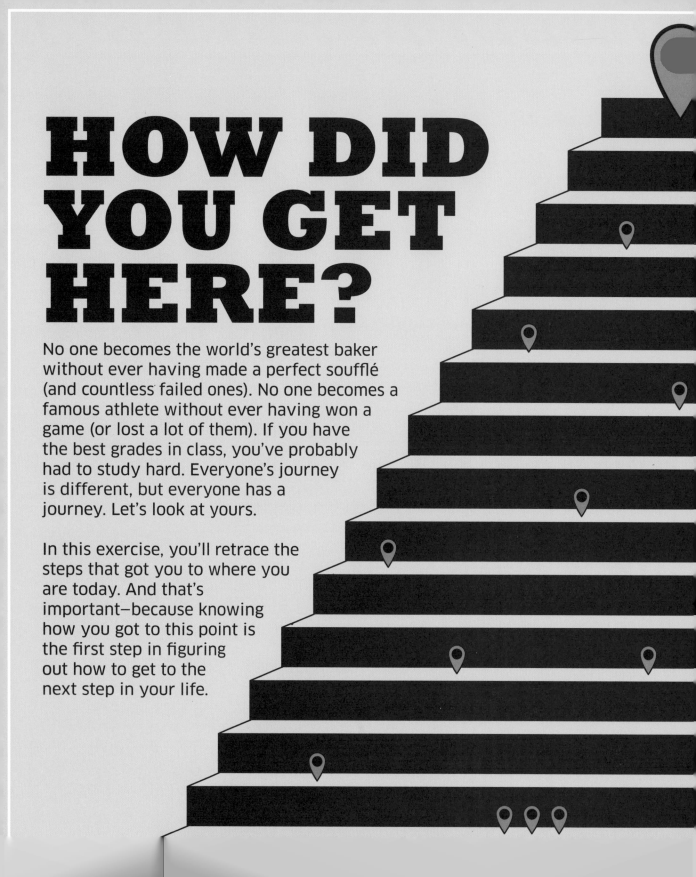

First, think of something you've accomplished that you're proud of. Then try breaking down your journey into 3 steps that got you there. For example:

I MADE THE SCHOOL SOCCER TEAM!

1. I played soccer for 10 years, from the time I was really little.
2. I signed up for tryouts and practiced hard.
3. I totally rocked tryouts.

Can you break it down even further? List the **6 steps** that got you to where you are. For example:

I MADE THE SCHOOL SOCCER TEAM!

1. My mom signed me up for pee wee soccer when I was 4 years old.
2. I fell in love with soccer and played in the park every day.
3. I played on a rec team through elementary school.
4. I decided to try out for the school soccer team.
5. I signed up for tryouts and practiced hard.
6. I totally rocked tryouts.

Can you break it down into **10 steps**? **15**? How far can you go?

Once you can't break it down any further, think ahead: What's a future goal you have that's similar to the one you accomplished? What steps do you need to climb to get there?

PIECES
OF YOUR
PAST

One of us (OK, it's Allie) has a shoebox at home filled with items that, at first glance, look like junk: a rock that's crumbling into dirt, old movie stubs, a bracelet made of orange construction paper, a vaguely heart-shaped ball formed from melted pink wax. If someone found this shoebox, they might toss it in the garbage without a second thought. But the items in this box are so meaningful on a personal level. Each trinket represents a past experience and helps to conjure the fond memories associated with it.

What items from your past hold special memories for you? List and draw each item here, and think about the memory it represents and why it's meaningful.

If you don't have a memory box already, consider making one to hold your memory items. Start with a shoebox or cardboard box and decorate it in a way that makes you happy. You can come back to this box again and again when you want to remember the special moments in your life. Your future self will thank you!

Hello, Past You . . .

Use these pages to write a letter to yourself **10 years ago**. What words of advice and encouragement would you give your past self? What do you wish you had known?

~This~
CHAPTER
IS ABOUT YOUR
PRESENT

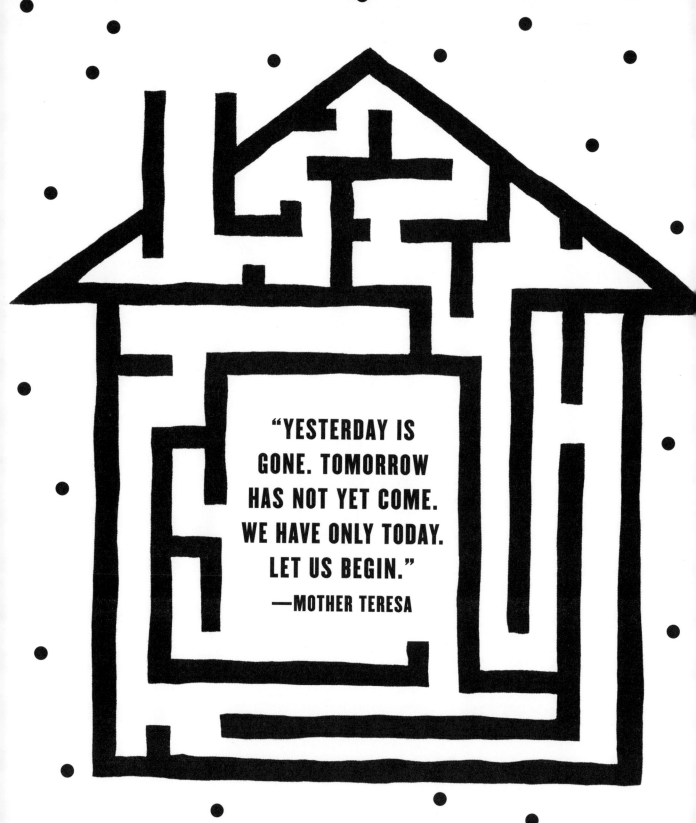

"YESTERDAY IS GONE. TOMORROW HAS NOT YET COME. WE HAVE ONLY TODAY. LET US BEGIN."

—MOTHER TERESA

NO PAST

NO FUTURE

JUST THIS

PERFECT

NOW

JACQUELINE WOODSON

Brown Girl Dreaming

YOUR Quirks AND Habits

Our quirks and habits are as unique as fingerprints—a whorl of everyday actions that are part of who we are. Dr. Seuss had a collection of over 100 hats, and he'd put one on any time he had writer's block. It's rumored that Katy Perry brushes her teeth six times a day (don't feel bad—we're lucky if we do it twice a day). Charles Dickens is thought to have combed his hair more than 100 times every day (he had Great Expectations for his comb . . .).

What are your personal quirks and habits? Do you have a lucky shirt that you absolutely must wear under your softball jersey for every home game? Do you have to read at least a few pages every night before falling asleep? Do you make sure your vegetables never touch the rice on your dinner plate?

FILL THIS PAGE WITH YOUR QUIRKS AND HABITS.

DESIGN YOUR PERFECT GOOD LUCK CHARM HERE.

"You know, Hobbes, some days even my lucky rocket ship underpants don't help."

—BILL WATTERSON, CREATOR OF "CALVIN AND HOBBES" COMIC STRIP

YOUR *Quirks* AND *Habits*

Describe a very ordinary
day from start to finish with as
much detail and drama as possible. For
example, "I awake with a start to a buzzing sound
coming from my nightstand. 'More sleep!' I shout, before
pushing the snooze button and ducking back under the warm
knit turquoise blanket. Not a minute later, a violent knocking at the
door, 'Get up! In the shower! You cannot be late again today!'
Mom can be incredibly dramatic at 7 a.m.
I wake up. . . ."

YOUR PRIMO PALS

Friends are some of the most important people in our lives.
They're there for us when things are going great, and when things get tricky or tough. Choosing the people you tell your secrets to, and who you want by your side, is a huge decision to make. How do you choose your fabulous friends? Answer the questions below.

What are the most important qualities you look for in a friend?

....
....
....
....

What are your favorite activities to do with your friends?

....
....
....
....

> *"I have friends I've known since I was seven. They have been there for all the weird moments and memories. They're like my family."*
>
> —NATALIE, 14

How often do you like to see your friends?

....
....
....
....

Is there someone you consider to be your best friend?

....
....
....
....

Which friend have you known the longest? Where did you meet him or her?

....
....
....
....

Are your friends a lot like you, or are they very different?

....
....
....
....

Has your friend group stayed the same, or has it changed over time?

....
....
....
....

Was there ever a time your friendships were challenged? What did you do?

....
....
....
....

What's the nicest thing a friend has ever done for you?

....
....
....
....

What's the nicest thing you've ever done for a friend?

....
....
....
....

YOUR PRIMO PALS

CONTINUED

"My friends always support each other, no matter what."

—PEYTON, 17

"I don't have a best friend. I have a group of friends, and I love them and the time we spend together."

—VICTORIA, 16

"Some friendships may not last forever, but they are wonderful to have."

—ALEX, 15

"My friends are amazing! I know I can always confide in them."

—JOIE, 12

"I love playing lacrosse with my friends."

—EDDIE, 13

"I only have a few friends, but they are very important to me."

—SARAH, 15

"My best friend and I grew up together and she knows me better than anyone."

—LAUREN, 13

"My cousins are my best friends. We go on big family vacations together."

—AMANDA, 16

What do *you* think about friendships?

"

"

What do *you* think about friendships?

"

"

What do *you* think about friendships?

"

"

What does your *friend* think about friendships?

"

"

What does your *friend* think about friendships?

"

"

EVALUATING YOUR
Friendships

On the previous few pages, you celebrated your amazing friendships. But what does it really mean to have good friends, and to be a good friend? What happens when good friendships go bad? Friendships are alive and dynamic; things change and people grow. Sometimes you may find yourself taking a step back and evaluating how things are.

Think of a friend, then answer "Yes" or "No" for each of the following descriptions to see how your friendships are going. (You can do this activity a number of times with different friends in mind.) When you've finished, turn the page for some expert advice.

1 Do you feel like you can be yourself around your friend?
○ **YES** ○ **NO**
Do you think your friend can be themselves around you?
○ **YES** ○ **NO**

2 Can you tell your friend anything without them judging or betraying you?
○ **YES** ○ **NO**
Can your friend tell you anything without you judging or betraying them?
○ **YES** ○ **NO**

3 Does your friend stay connected with you, even when they are busy?
○ **YES** ○ **NO**
Do you stay connected with your friend, even when you are busy?
○ **YES** ○ **NO**

4 Does your friend ever pressure you, or make you feel bad about yourself?
○ **YES** ○ **NO**
Do you ever pressure your friend, or make them feel bad about themselves?
○ **YES** ○ **NO**

5 Do you worry that your friend will make new friends, leaving you behind?
○ **YES** ○ **NO**
Do you think your friend worries about you making new friends and leaving them behind?
○ **YES** ○ **NO**

6 Does your friend always get to make the decisions or take all of the attention in your friendship?
○ **YES** ○ **NO**
Do you always get to make the decisions or take all of the attention in your friendship?
○ **YES** ○ **NO**

WITH THE EVALUATION DONE, IT'S TIME FOR SOME ADVICE FROM AN EXPERT.

 STAYING TRUE TO YOURSELF: You should never have to change or censor yourself around those closest to you. This doesn't mean you can be mean to someone just because you're being "honest." But you should feel like you're your truest self and be able to speak most honestly around your closest friends.

 TRUSTING EACH OTHER: Friends should make each other feel comfortable and confident when they're sharing their thoughts and feelings. Friends accept each other as they are, and don't tease or belittle one another's feelings.

 STAYING CONNECTED: It only takes 10 seconds to send a text saying, "Miss you, can't wait to catch up when things settle down!" It makes all the difference to let people know you're thinking of them. It also builds trust and support.

 HELPING, NOT CONTROLLING: Friendly advice can be fun, but make sure you or your friend are not being bossy, controlling, or rude. Friends are there to help each other, not to take control or make their friend feel bad.

 BEING A LOYAL FRIEND: Trust, honor, and loyalty are the cornerstones of a strong friendship. If you doubt a friend, is it because you have trouble trusting people, or is your friend doing something to cause you to doubt them?

 KEEPING THINGS EQUAL: True friendships, at heart, must always be equal. One person may be more outgoing or more assertive, but at the end of the day, no one person should be "in charge" or be thought of as more "valuable" than the other.

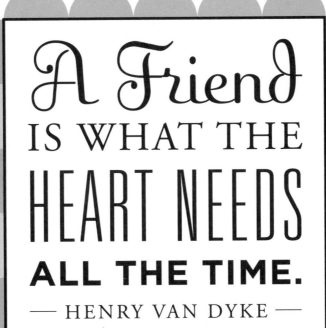

A Friend IS WHAT THE HEART NEEDS ALL THE TIME.

— HENRY VAN DYKE —

YOU DO YOU!

EXERCISE 1:

CRAZY FUN!

Choose your favorite fun song (something silly like "Jumpshot" by Dawin). Turn off the lights, raise the volume up, and MOVE. Just have fun being you. Feel the instruments while you listen to the words as you move, move, move!

Jaquetta Perry is a strong woman who inspires us. She's a speech-language specialist so she understands the deep value of self expression. She also happens to be an amazing dancer and a certified Zumba instructor who believes that dancing can be a powerful path to expression, happiness, and FUN!

Here are Jaquetta's top four tips to get you up and dancing (even if your moves are not quite Beyoncé-like):

EXERCISE 2:
SLITHER AND SWAY

Find your favorite spicy song (something like "Hips Don't Lie" by Shakira or "Dangerous Woman" by Ariana Grande). This time, dim the lights (everything looks more awesome in dim light) and look at yourself in the mirror while you sway your body from left to right. Relax and love your body from the inside out. Sway, sway, sway!

YOU DO YOU!

EXERCISE 3:

HAPPY! HAPPY!

Choose a song that makes you feel happy (something like "Don't Want to Know" by Maroon 5 or "Happy" by Pharrel Williams). Find that song that brings you absolute joy each time you hear it. Dance your way. Dance your style. Smile, laugh, breathe, and have fun! Groove, groove, groove to your happy tune.

CRAZY POWER

Find your favorite tune that makes you forget all about your troubles (think "Dancing Queen" by ABBA or "Fight Song" by Rachel Platten or "Hall of Fame" by The Script). Find a tune that is crazy and fun. Just let go! Let your body move without any expectations from yourself. You may clap, jump, scream while you breathe in the new air and push out the old. Lose, lose, lose yourself to the music.

A STYLE ALL YOUR OWN

Here's a throwback to paper dolls. Style the figures you see here with the clothes and accessories YOU would wear for each occasion. Use colored pencils, magazine cutouts, glitter—anything you want.

If you're not usually a fashionista, that's OK. Try anyway. You're going to need to wear something when you get your Oscar for cinematography, so you should start thinking about it now.

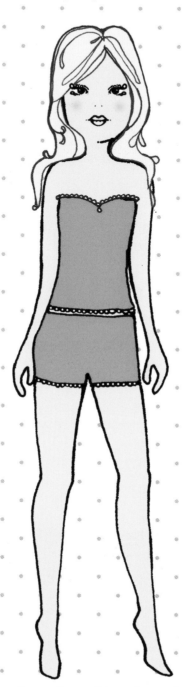

A Lazy Day at Home

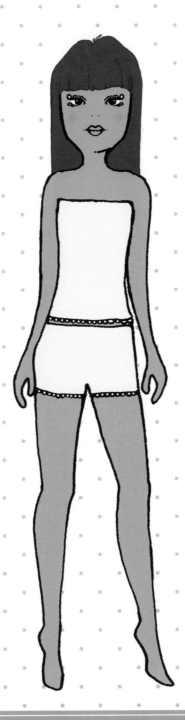

You're Going to the Oscars!

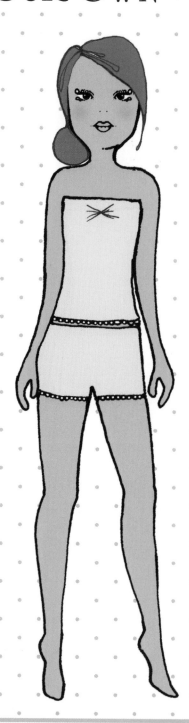

Inauguration Day, and You're the President

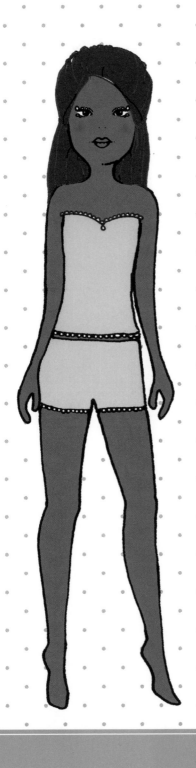

Insert Your Own Idea Here

A FEW OF YOUR *Favorite* THINGS

For Maria, it was raindrops on roses and whiskers on kittens. Rumor has it she was also fond of bright copper kettles, warm woolen mittens, and brown paper packages tied up with string. (Really, brown paper and string? Girlfriend was easy to please.)

If you haven't seen *The Sound of Music*, sorry—you can ignore all that. The point is, we all have our favorite things: the items that make us smile and feel all warm inside. What are yours? Fill in each heart on these pages with an item that brings you joy. You can write it down, draw it, or paste in a photo or magazine clipping of it.

A FEW OF YOUR *Favorite* THINGS

CONTINUED

Now that you've filled in the previous page with your favorite objects, let's take it a step further: On this page, fill in each cloud with an intangible thing that brings you joy. It could be a feeling, a thought, a belief, a hope, or anything else you can't physically see or hold in your hand. If that's not enough of a challenge, can you draw it, or find a photo to represent it?

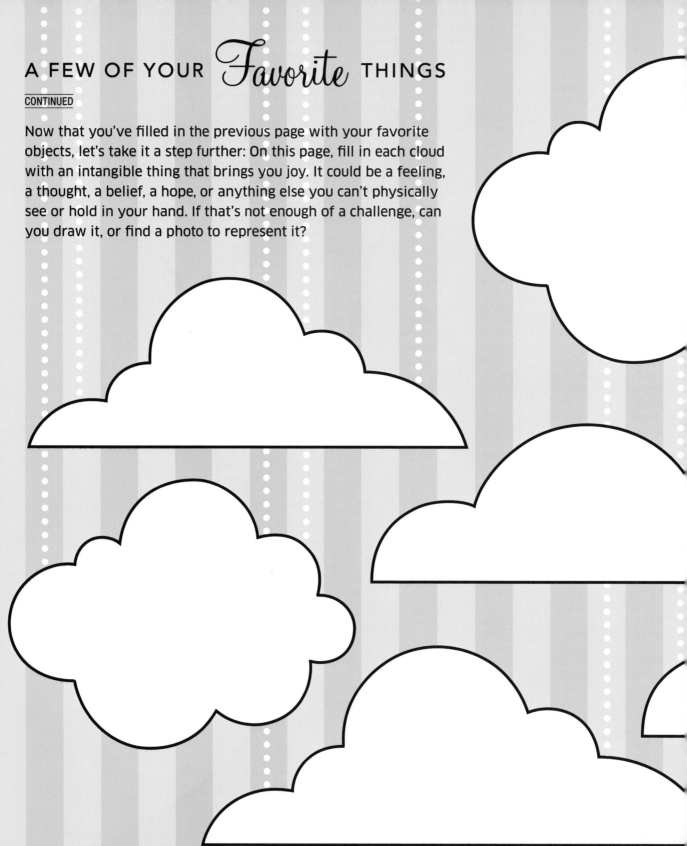

★ ★ ★ WHAT'S ★ ★ ★
IMPORTANT
TO YOU NOW?

It's hard to balance school, friends, family, and all the other fun stuff you'd like to pack into a day. So you make choices about what matters most—whether that's getting straight As, checking in with a friend, or never missing lacrosse practice. Try this quiz to find out more.

YOUR IDEA OF A PERFECT FRIDAY NIGHT:

❏ **A.** Theater practice, then head over to the animal shelter to volunteer in the cat room.

❏ **B.** Go to your cousin's house for pizza and a movie.

❏ **C.** Study. All the time. Just study.

❏ **D.** Go to the high school football game and cheer on your team!

YOUR GRANDPARENTS ARE COMING TO STAY WITH YOUR FAMILY FOR A WEEK. HOW DO YOU REACT?

❏ **A.** That's awesome! We have a big band concert that week and they can come!

❏ **B.** I can't wait! I think I'll make a welcome banner for them with my brother.

❏ **C.** I'm excited to see them, but I have a huge test coming up. Maybe they can help me with my flash cards?

❏ **D.** I wonder if grandpa is any good at playing kickball?

IF YOU SIGN UP FOR CHORUS THIS YEAR, IT MEANS YOU DON'T GET A LUNCH PERIOD. WHAT DO YOU DO?

❑ **A.** Absolutely. Lunch is for boring people. I'll have a big breakfast.

❑ **B.** It would be really hard to skip lunch— that's when I get a chance to hang out with my friends.

❑ **C.** Chorus would look good on my college application, but I do like to use lunchtime to read ahead for history class.

❑ **D.** The track team runs sprints during lunch a few times a week, and I don't think I could make it work.

EVERY SUNDAY YOUR FAMILY PICKS A MOVIE TO WATCH, AND IT'S FINALLY YOUR TURN TO CHOOSE! YOUR SELECTION IS:

❑ **A.** *Grease*

❑ **B.** *Star Wars*

❑ **C.** *Akeelah and the Bee*

❑ **D.** *The Sandlot*

WHICH OF THESE PEOPLE DO YOU ADMIRE THE MOST?

❑ **A.** Neil Patrick Harris

❑ **B.** Beyoncé

❑ **C.** Bill Gates

❑ **D.** Venus and Serena Williams

FOR EXTRA CREDIT (AND YOU WANT THAT EXTRA CREDIT) YOUR CIVICS TEACHER WILL LET YOU WORK ON A VOLUNTEER PROJECT. WHICH LOCAL CHARITY PROJECT DO YOU CHOOSE TO WORK ON?

❑ **A.** The nursing home in town is looking for students who can entertain the residents with music.

❑ **B.** Your whole family volunteers at a local soup kitchen, so that's a perfect fit.

❑ **C.** Tutoring elementary-school kids in math.

❑ **D.** Helping coach the Special Olympics.

If you chose mostly As, you're an **EXTRA-CURRICULAR EXTRAORDINAIRE.**

You can't stand to have an empty calendar—you're always joining a new club, auditioning for the school play, or volunteering to take pictures for the yearbook. It's great that you like to keep busy, but make sure you're still keeping some time for yourself to chill out and relax.

If you chose mostly Bs, you're **FRIENDS AND FAMILY FOCUSED.**

There's nothing you love more than hanging out with the people you love. Family time is never a chore for you—you actually think your parents are kind of cool. But don't forget that it's also good to meet new people and try new things. Sometimes it's easy to get comfortable hanging out with the same folks all the time.

If you chose mostly Cs, you're an ACADEMIC ACHIEVER.

You just don't understand why other people don't study as much as you do—you've been thinking about college and SAT scores since third grade. You love learning and push yourself academically. In the quest to be the best, try to remember that your brain needs a break sometimes. It's OK to spend a Saturday watching movies with your friends or listening to music.

If you chose mostly Ds, you're a SPORT AND FITNESS FANATIC.

You go for the gold every day, challenging yourself to run faster, jump higher, and work harder in the gym and on the field. You put your team and your coach second only to your family. It's terrific that you've found your niche, but don't forget to spend some time relaxing off the field with your family or a good book or anything else that will help you relax and use another part of your brain. You can have it all!

FACE YOUR FEARS

A big part of growing up involves trying new things. Some people LOVE trying new foods, going to new places, meeting new people, and having new experiences. Others, however, feel more at home sticking to what they know. Either way, at some point, we are all forced to face new—sometimes scary—situations. Exploring how you face things that are intimidating or overwhelming is a great way to learn how you can succeed in even the scariest situation. The better you understand why you're nervous or afraid, the better you can work with and through your fears.

WHAT MAKES YOU THE MOST AFRAID?
ASSIGN A POINT VALUE FROM 1 TO 5 TO EACH OF THE FOLLOWING.

1 = I'M NOT AFRAID. I CAN TOTALLY HANDLE IT.
5 = I'M SO AFRAID, I CAN'T EVEN THINK ABOUT IT.

- [ ] Starting a new school in a new place where you don't know anyone

- [ ] Riding in a car with someone who is driving way too fast on a dark, curvy road

- [ ] Giving a speech in front of a large crowd

- [ ] Learning that someone you care about has become sick

- [ ] Bungee-jumping off an enormous bridge

- [ ] Exploring a cave filled with bats, snakes, spiders, and other creepy crawlies

- [ ] Playing in the big championship game, or starring in a major performance

- [ ] Taking a final exam in your most difficult subject

- [ ] Finding out your friends have planned a vacation and didn't invite you

FACE YOUR FEARS

Add up your point values from the previous page by color. There are three red scenarios, three blue scenarios, and three green scenarios. What type of fear plagues you the most?

☐ / 15 **SELF-PROTECTION FEARS:** These are fears of dangerous situations that could cause bodily harm. There's no wonder the brain tries to stop us from getting too close to a snake or falling from an unsafe height. If you scored high on this type of fear, it doesn't mean you have to stay away from adventure. It just means you'll be very careful in choosing which risks are worth taking.

☐ / 15 **SEPARATION FEARS:** No matter how confident you are, or how much you enjoy independent time, humans are meant to be around other humans. We all have a need to feel approved, accepted, and respected. Threats to our feelings of belonging—from losing a loved one to being left out of a group activity—can cause fear. If you scored high on this section, don't worry. The need to be connected is one we all share.

☐ / 15 **SELF-APPROVAL FEARS:** As much as we need approval from others, we equally need approval from ourselves! Anything that causes a sense of unworthiness or shame, such as failing a test or performing poorly in a major sports event, can trigger fear. The more you accept and forgive yourself, the better you can face your fears! Remember, making mistakes doesn't mean you're not worthy, it means you're human.

Give one or more of these methods a try next time you find yourself in a scary situation. Which method works best for you?

VISUALIZATION: Picture the fear in your mind as clearly as you can. (It works!)

EXPOSURE: The more you experience something, the less scary it will seem.

BABY STEPS: You don't have to conquer a whole fear at once. Take it one small step at a time.

PEP TALKS: Whether from a friend or talking to yourself in the mirror, you need to hear "You can do it!"

ACCURACY EVALUATION: Are you scared of something that, honestly, just isn't going to happen?

RISK EVALUATION: How safe is the situation? What are the true risks?

BENEFIT EVALUATION: Is the thing you're afraid of even worth doing? What are the benefits?

RELAX!

When facing fear, your body has a physical reaction. The central nervous system speeds up, causing a faster heartbeat, sweating, rising blood pressure, and heightened anxiety. Relaxation exercises help calm the nervous system and lessen fear. (This is why people count to 10 and take deep breaths in challenging situations!) Try it now: Close your eyes, stretch your hands above your head, and take a deep breath, in and out. Do this five times. On each exhale, lower your arms and release any stressful thoughts you might be having. Even this simple activity can make you feel lighter and calmer.

SAMPLE SITUATION: Are you uncomfortable being the center of attention? Try these tools. **Baby steps:** Tell a familiar, funny story the next time you're with friends. **Exposure:** Watch people stay calm when they're in the spotlight. If they can do it, so can you! **Visualization:** Picture yourself hitting the ball at the big game, singing in front of an audience, or giving a great speech. Each time you visualize a situation, it gets a little less scary.

HOW DO YOU FEEL?

Emotions are meant to guide you, even if some emotions are more comfortable to experience than others. It's easy to feel happy, for instance, but every emotion (even those that don't seem so great) has a time, place, and purpose. Whether you're a very emotional person or consider yourself to be totally chill, understanding your different moods and emotions is a very powerful tool.

Are you feeling up to an activity? Here's how it works:

- Read each of the words on the next page aloud, one by one.
- As you read each word, try to recall a time you felt that emotion really strongly.
- If you can EASILY recall a time you felt that emotion, circle it. If you can't, don't.
- When you're finished, turn the page to learn what your answers could mean.

Safe	Resentful	Angry
Accepted	Relieved	Shocked
Rejected	Aggressive	Confident
Guilty	Afraid	Smug
Impressed	Vulnerable	Disapproving
Impressive	Grateful	Strong
Inadequate	Shy	Elated
Excited	Loved	Manipulated
Apathetic	Excluded	Idealistic
Satisfied	Jealous	Passionate
Isolated	Uncomfortable	Happy
Charming	Overwhelmed	Sad

HOW DO YOU **FEEL?**

CONTINUED

How many of your circled emotions brought up negative memories? How many brought up positive memories? (That's right, go back and count. We'll wait.)

What patterns do you see in your answers? (There is no right or wrong.) We all have "emotional habits" in the way we think and react. If you tend toward negative answers, this may mean you are selective and have high, hard-to-please standards that drive you toward your goals. But does it mean you can be too hard on yourself or on others? Perhaps you could use a bit of mellowing out? Negative answers also may show that you tend to feel your emotions deeply, which can be great. But be sure to welcome enough lightheartedness in your life.

Do you tend to have a lot of positive answers? It is wonderful to be optimistic and appreciative of the good things out there. But does it mean that are you missing out on seeing what lies below the surface? Do you have a healthy grasp of reality, or do you sometimes see only what you want to see? The deepest growth often occurs from things that are hardest to go through. Usually people find a balance between a glass that is half empty and one that is half full, but being aware of our own tendencies can always help us better understand ourselves and others.

How are you feeling right now? One of the best ways to find out is to free write. Set a timer for two minutes and just let loose. Write down on this page everything you're thinking and feeling this very moment. Ready, set, GO.

GO WITH YOUR GUT:

TIRED OF ALL THE THINKING THIS BOOK IS MAKING YOU DO? IT'S TIME TO GO WITH YOUR GUT. CIRCLE YOUR ANSWERS BELOW:
WOULD YOU RATHER . . .

HAVE A **DAILY ROUTINE**

OR

DO THINGS **DIFFERENTLY** EVERY DAY?

BE GOOD AT **A LOT OF SPORTS** **OR** BE AMAZING IN **ONE SPORT?**

HAVE A **BIG GROUP** OF FRIENDS

OR

HAVE **ONE** BEST FRIEND?

OWN **A LOT OF OUTFITS** YOU LIKE

OR

OWN **A FEW OUTFITS** YOU LOVE?

AVOID THE THINGS YOU'RE SCARED OF

OR

CONQUER YOUR FEARS?

PLAY A MUSICAL **INSTRUMENT** **OR** GO TO A **CONCERT?**

BE **IDEALISTIC** **OR** BE **REALISTIC?**

PRESENT

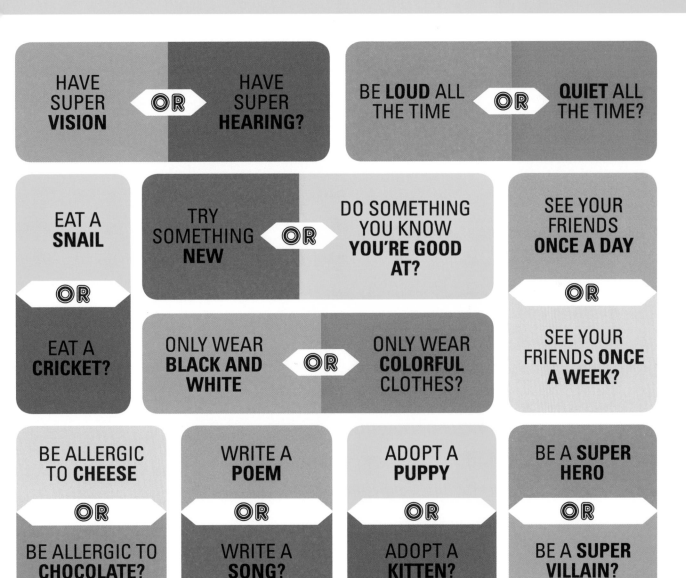

HAVE SUPER **VISION** **OR** HAVE SUPER **HEARING?**

BE **LOUD** ALL THE TIME **OR** **QUIET** ALL THE TIME?

EAT A **SNAIL** **OR** EAT A **CRICKET?**

TRY SOMETHING **NEW** **OR** DO SOMETHING YOU KNOW **YOU'RE GOOD AT?**

SEE YOUR FRIENDS **ONCE A DAY** **OR** SEE YOUR FRIENDS **ONCE A WEEK?**

ONLY WEAR **BLACK AND WHITE** **OR** ONLY WEAR **COLORFUL** CLOTHES?

BE ALLERGIC TO **CHEESE** **OR** BE ALLERGIC TO **CHOCOLATE?**

WRITE A **POEM** **OR** WRITE A **SONG?**

ADOPT A **PUPPY** **OR** ADOPT A **KITTEN?**

BE A **SUPER HERO** **OR** BE A **SUPER VILLAIN?**

advice
you can use right now

...

We asked some of the strong women we know for advice that you, yes you!,
can use right this second. Here's what they had to say.

Stay out of the drama your friends might put you in. **VERONICA M.**

Stick with your clubs and activities. Those skills and commitments will push you into more positive and enriching circles. Stop being the outsider! **RACHEL R.**

There is so much more to life than boys. **SUZANNE J.**

Don't be so quick to want to be "grown up." There are so many things you get to do before you grow up—so do them and enjoy them. And take naps. You will miss them when you grow up. Trust me. **TAMMY O.**

Work at your self-esteem, it will stand you in good stead. (And always seek your own approval above that of others.) **SADIE S.**

Have more fun. Way more. **JILL C.**

Listen to your "uh-oh" voice. Get to know it well. Learn to trust it. It will lead you away from things which will be time suckers and toward better things. **DEANNA R.**

What most people think about you really doesn't matter. Retain your own power. You know your own story best. **LAURIE S.**

Standing up for yourself is never the wrong way to go. **MACKENZIE F.**

It's OK to be single. MICHELLE B.

Don't say no to any opportunity. You have no idea where it will take you. TAMMY O.

Hey you. You, deep down in there, right now. Loving, crazy, yearning you in there, right now, with all you know and feel to date: You're RIGHT. Trust yourself and GO. Give 'em all the love and hell you've got to give. BARB S.

NEVER let yourself be defined by what a guy thinks of you. You are better than that. ERIN B.

You won't always end up where you THOUGHT you'd be, but you'll always end up where you were MEANT to be. TRACY C.

Try not to JUDGE others. You never know what is really going on inside someone else. SUSAN M.

Be the person who never speaks negatively about others. JENAFER M.

Never stop reading or traveling. They will both make you wise and help you see how small you are. BETH W.

There is no finish line. There is no point when you stop wanting to be better. And that's good. KATHY J.

Don't be afraid to stand out. LAINA J.

Write all the special things down. You think you'll remember them but you won't. RACHEL K.

Spend as much time as you can with your parents. LAURIE B.

Don't pretend to like something you don't just because you think it will make some boy (or girl) like you. Either they like you for who you are, or they don't. And if they don't, move on.

COLLEEN C.

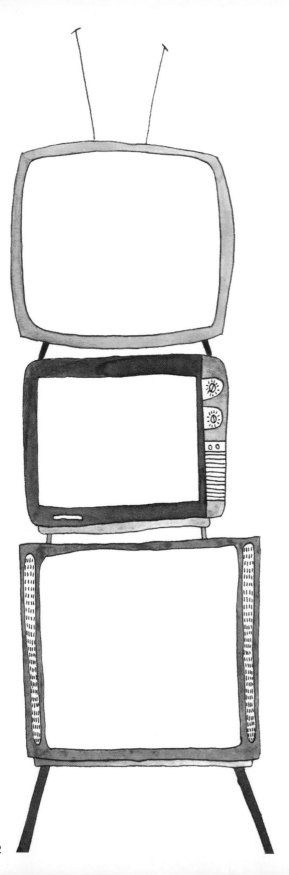

COMING AT YOU!

YOU'VE HEARD THE EXPRESSION, "YOU ARE WHAT YOU EAT," RIGHT? YOU'RE ALSO WHAT YOU READ, WATCH, PLAY, AND HEAR. TAKE SOME TIME TO RECORD AND REFLECT ON THE MEDIA YOU CONSUME EVERY DAY.

List your top three favorite television shows.

1. ....

2. ....

3. ....

What is it that keeps you watching?

....

....

....

....

....

What film have you watched the most times?
(Note: One of us has seen *Harry Potter and the Sorcerer's Stone* 20+ times. We're not naming names.)

....

Why can you watch it over and over?

....

....

....

....

What are the three best films you've watched this year?

1. ....
2. ....
3. ....

Why did you pick them? Did they make you happy? Sad? Did they inspire you to learn more about something?

....
....
....
....

What are the top three YouTube videos you've watched?

1. ....
2. ....
3. ....

Why do you like them? Are they funny? Clever? Full of useful information?

....
....
....

What is your all-time favorite band or singer?

....

How did you find them? What are the specific things you love about their music?

....
....
....

If you could only play 5 songs over and over again for all eternity, what would they be?

1. ....
2. ....
3. ....
4. ....
5. ....

What three books do you love the most?

1. ....
2. ....
3. ....

Is there a book you reread every year? Or that you'd like to reread every year? Explain— and write down a quote or two from that book that you love.

....
....
....
....
....
....

THE SPOTLIGHT'S ON YOU

Imagine: You're suddenly famous, and everyone wants a piece of you. Hollywood's calling, Broadway's emailing, publishing houses are knocking down your door . . . . Time to make some demands, you diva you.

Who would play you in a movie about your life?

What kind of movie would it be? (comedy, drama, romance . . .)

Who would play you in a TV show about your life?

What would the TV show be called?

Who would be your date to the movie premiere?

What websites, YouTube channels, or magazines would you do interviews with?

What would the title of the book be?

Who would play you in a Broadway show about your life?

What author would write a book about your life?

Would the show be a play (a comedy or a drama?) or a musical?

What musician or band would write and play a song about your life?

What kind of song would it be? (fast, slow, happy, sad . . .)

EXPRESS YOURSELF

You express yourself every day just by being you. The clothes you wear, the way you carry yourself, the people you hang out with, the books you read: it's all YOU.

There's another very deliberate way you can express yourself—through art. Even if you think you're not a great artist, that shouldn't stop you from trying. No one needs to see or read anything you do—it's YOUR book. Take a deep breath and let your creativity flow.

COMPOSE A SHORT SONG.

Ideas to get you started:
• The happiest day you've ever had
• A special person in your life
• The best place you've ever visited (your Grandma's house on Long Island, a baseball game in Chicago, a park down the street from your best friend's house)

"Music was my refuge. I could crawl into the space between the notes and curl my back to loneliness." –**MAYA ANGELOU**

"You are so busy being YOU that you have no idea how utterly unprecedented you are."

—JOHN GREEN
The Fault in Our Stars

EXPRESS YOURSELF

CONTINUED

WRITE A POEM.
Ideas to get you started:
• A description of your favorite season
• Your favorite meal, with every delicious taste and smell
• An acrostic poem using the letters of your first name (What's an acrostic poem, you ask? Google it. Just kidding. It's a poem where the first letter of every line spells out a word or a phrase.)

"If I read a book and it makes my whole body so cold no fire can ever warm me, I know that is poetry."
—EMILY DICKINSON

"Drawing is still basically the same as it has been since prehistoric times. It brings together man and the world. It lives through magic."
–KEITH HARING

YOUR LIFE, THE EXPERIMENT

The scientific method is a series of steps that scientists use to try to answer questions about how our world works. Maybe you've used it before in your science class. But have you ever thought about applying it to personal situations? We all make big decisions that involve heightened emotions—nervousness, fear, uncertainty. Sometimes putting on your science brain and treating your life like a science experiment can help you see a clear solution.

▾ THIS IS HOW IT'S DONE:

 ASK A QUESTION

"What do I want to be when I grow up?"

 DO BACKGROUND RESEARCH

"What skills do I have? What do I love to do? Where do I want to live? What are my career options?"

 CONSTRUCT A HYPOTHESIS

"I want to be a marine biologist."

 TEST WITH AN EXPERIMENT

Sign up for a marine biology summer camp.

 DID IT WORK?

YES: "I had an amazing time and did a great job."
NO: "I didn't like working with the animals at the camp. And I got seasick."

 IF YES, **ANALYZE DATA AND DRAW CONCLUSIONS**

"I know I was good with the animals, and I loved what I was doing. I want to be a marine biologist."

IF NO, **MAKE A NEW HYPOTHESIS**

"What other skills do I have? What else do I love to do?"

 SHARE YOUR RESULTS AND PLAN OUT NEXT STEPS

Tell your parents or a school counselor, and begin looking for marine biology programs or courses at other camps or colleges.

Use the templates on the next pages to try it out yourself.
DON'T FORGET TO RECORD YOUR FINDINGS! ➤

YOUR LIFE, **THE EXPERIMENT**

<u>CONTINUED</u>

 ASK A QUESTION

 DO BACKGROUND RESEARCH

 CONSTRUCT A HYPOTHESIS

 TEST WITH AN EXPERIMENT

 DID IT WORK?

 IF YES, **ANALYZE DATA AND DRAW CONCLUSIONS**

 IF NO, **MAKE A NEW HYPOTHESIS**

 SHARE YOUR RESULTS AND PLAN OUT NEXT STEPS

ASK A QUESTION

 DO BACKGROUND RESEARCH

 CONSTRUCT A HYPOTHESIS

 TEST WITH AN EXPERIMENT

 DID IT WORK?

 IF YES, **ANALYZE DATA AND DRAW CONCLUSIONS**

 IF NO, **MAKE A NEW HYPOTHESIS**

 SHARE YOUR RESULTS AND PLAN OUT NEXT STEPS

OPPOSITE YOU

IT'S OPPOSITE DAY! (OK, NOT A REAL HOLIDAY, BUT LET'S PRETEND.)

ANSWER THE QUESTIONS BELOW PRETENDING THAT YOU'RE THE OPPOSITE-DAY VERSION OF YOURSELF. FOR INSTANCE, IF YOU HATE PARTIES AND YOU'RE A VEGETARIAN IN REAL LIFE, YOU MIGHT SAY:

This weekend I spent all Saturday at _JoJo's pool party_. I had the best time _talking to strangers_ and _eating hot dogs_.

Some days I just want to come home from school, make myself a delicious snack of _____ and turn on my favorite show, _____.

When I grow up, I definitely want to be a _____. Everyone knows I love _____ and_____, so it makes perfect sense.

My parents are buying us a pet _____!!! I can't wait to _____ it!

If I had to pick one favorite memory from my life so far, it would definitely be the time _____ _____.

There's no subject better than _____. I find the whole subject _____ and I can't wait to do my homework every night.

I have an idea for dinner: Let's have _____ with a side of _____. Can you imagine anything more delicious?

We just won a vacation to _____. Two weeks of _____ and _____. Time to pack my _____!

OPPOSITE YOU

OPPOSITE YOU

OPPOSITE DAY IS OVER. ANSWER THE SAME QUESTIONS LIKE YOUR NORMAL, REGULAR, NOT-THE-OPPOSITE SELF!

This weekend I spent all Saturday _____. I had the best time _____ and _____.

Some days I just want to come home from school, make myself a delicious snack of _____ and turn on my favorite show, _____.

When I grow up, I definitely want to be a _____. Everyone knows I love _____ and _____, so it makes perfect sense.

My parents are buying us a pet _____!!! I can't wait to _____ it!

If I had to pick one favorite memory from my life so far, it would definitely be the time _____ _____.

There's no subject better than _____. I find the whole subject _____ and I can't wait to do my homework every night.

I have an idea for dinner: Let's have _____ with a side of _____. Can you imagine anything more delicious?

We just won a vacation to _____. Two weeks of _____ and _____. Time to pack my _____!

IT'S YOUR SPACE

Your space reflects you—and space could mean your room, your backpack, or your shelf in the bathroom. Take this quick quiz to learn more about your personal space style.

Do you make your bed every morning before you leave for school?

❑ **A.** Absolutely—and you can bounce a quarter off the sheets.

❑ **B.** Make the bed? I don't do that.

❑ **C.** Almost every day—if I don't hit snooze an extra time or two.

You're getting ready to go out to the movies with your friends. How easy is it to find the exact outfit you'd like to wear?

❑ **A.** Is this a trick question? The closet. Where else would I keep my freshly pressed clothes.

❑ **B.** I'm hoping the pants are somewhere on the bed. The shirt's in the hamper, but there's nothing a little Febreze can't fix.

❑ **C.** Mom just dropped off a clean pile of laundry, so I'm pretty confident the dress I'm looking for is there.

Your best friend is coming over in an hour. How much time do you spend getting your room picture perfect?

❑ **A.** It's already there—but I might do a little last-minute dusting to make it shine.

❑ **B.** A hour? That's about enough time for me to shove everything into the closet and make the bed, but I'll still try to steer her into the living room instead.

❑ **C.** Maybe 30 minutes—it could use a little vacuuming and dusting.

Reading rocks. How do you organize your books?

❑ **A.** Dewey decimal system, all the way.

❑ **B.** They're everywhere: the bed, the nightstand, the floor, the dining room table. But I know where to find them when I need them.

❑ **C.** They're on a shelf, mostly. (Does my nightstand count as a shelf?)

Quick! You need to look over last week's homework to get ready for a quiz. Where do you find it?

- ❏ **A.** It's in my three-ring binder in the "Homework" section, of course.
- ❏ **B.** Uh oh, I'm gonna have to wing it. I think I used that homework as a napkin.
- ❏ **C.** It's definitely somewhere in my backpack.

How many toiletries do you keep on the bathroom sink?

- ❏ **A.** None. I have them in baskets in the linen closet.
- ❏ **B.** All of them. So. Much. Lotion.
- ❏ **C.** Just the toothpaste and my hair stuff. And only until my mom clears it all off and puts it in my room.

Accessories—we all have too many of them. Headbands, scarves, necklaces, earrings. What's your style for keeping them all together?

- ❏ **A.** I've got a jewelry armoire that keeps it all organized by style, shape, and color.
- ❏ **B.** I keep them together in a big ball at the bottom of my closet.
- ❏ **C.** My nice jewelry is in a cool jewelry box. The rest is scattered around my room.

You just unwrapped a piece of gum. Where do you put the wrapper?

- ❏ **A.** In the trash. Seriously, is this a trick question?
- ❏ **B.** My pockets are full of wrappers, so this would join the rest.
- ❏ **C.** If there's a garbage can nearby, I'd put it there. If not I'd probably stick it in my purse.

Instagram. Snapchat. YouTube. How organized is your tech?

- ❏ **A.** I have a clear desktop, my photos are sorted by month and year, and my cell phone apps are organized by usefulness. I've got this.
- ❏ **B.** It's all a great big mess. I'm grateful for "Search."
- ❏ **C.** I can find what I need, but I wish I had time to organize my 10,005 photos!

Your awesome aunt bought you an amazing print off Etsy (you can't resist any picture of a cat in a sweater vest). How do you display it?

- ❏ **A.** Professionally framed and proudly hung over the bed.
- ❏ **B.** There's a good chance I'll forget to hang it up until I know my aunt is coming over—then I'll tack it up on my bulletin board or tape it up on the wall.
- ❏ **C.** Repurpose an old frame that's almost the same size.

IT'S YOUR SPACE

CONTINUED

Mostly As:
NEAT AND TIDY

Your room is neat as a pin—your parents never even ask if it's clean, because they know it's perfect. Your clothes are clean, ironed, and lint-free, and your backpack is organized by subject. You can't help it, staying neat and organized is just how you roll. You might want to cut yourself a little slack from time to time—it's great to help your parents with chores, but not so great that you panic at lunch if a drop of ketchup accidentally squirts on your T-shirt.

Mostly Bs:
PRETTY MESSY

There is a half-eaten pudding cup in your closet. You don't feel good about it, but you also don't feel inclined to throw it out. You've always been a little challenged when it comes to cleaning up, and there's no big sign of improvement. You only have one argument with your parents, and it's the same argument again and again: Why won't you clean your room? Look, it's OK to be a little sloppy, but you might find that a little organization goes a long way to improving your mood (less panic and rushing around to find things!) and your relationship with your folks.

Mostly Cs:
RIGHT IN THE MIDDLE

You love helping vacuum the house, but don't open your closet door—it's likely a tumble of shoes, books, and sweaters will fall out in a dramatic crash. You have aspirations to be neater and more organized, but sometimes a busy life—karate practice, movies, homework—gets in the way. Keep up the good fight, and maybe someday soon you can open up that closet without fear.

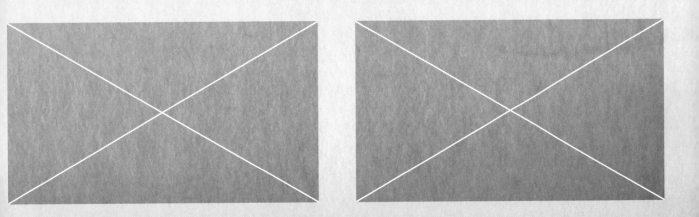

"THE OBJECTIVE OF CLEANING IS NOT JUST TO CLEAN, BUT TO FEEL HAPPINESS LIVING WITHIN THAT ENVIRONMENT."
—MARIE KONDO, *The Life-Changing Magic of Tidying Up*

"The worst enemy to creativity is self-doubt."

—SYLVIA PLATH

BELIEVE IN YOURSELF

Do you know people who always seem sure of themselves? People who, no matter what the situation, always seem comfortable, know what to do, and what to say? What's their secret? And why don't you feel that way? These activities are about self-confidence no matter what your personality type.

Here are two tricky situations. First, write how you would handle each one, and then go to the bottom of this page for some expert analysis.

1. A close friend is afraid of flying. She just took her first plane ride from Florida to New York, and she is excited to tell you about it. However, you travel a lot and have been flying your whole life; to you, her short flight is no big deal. **What do you tell her?**

....
....
....
....
....
....
....
....
....

2. There's a new girl at school. She's gorgeous, in honors classes, good at sports, already hanging out with the most well-liked kids at school . . . all of the things you wish you could be. One day, you find her in the bathroom crying. **How do you feel?**

....
....
....
....
....
....
....
....
....

OUR EXPERT SAYS:

1. Would you support her, or brag about your own travel triumphs? A sign of **true self-confidence** is being able to celebrate other people's successes. Someone who is really self-confident is able to **show empathy** for someone else's experience. We all have fears to overcome! You don't need to show off your own strengths. If you decide to tell her about your experiences, make sure it is in a way that says, **"I can do it, and so can you."**

2. Would you **feel sad** that she's going through a hard time, or secretly kind of **happy** that she's not so perfect after all? A **truly self-confident** person feels good about herself no matter what. She doesn't need to see someone else in pain just to feel confident in herself. Seeing her classmate suffer should trigger **empathy**, not victory. A self-confident person is able to recognize that **no one is perfect**—no matter what it looks like on the outside—and **that's OK.**

BELIEVE IN YOURSELF
<u>CONTINUED</u>

What makes you feel like your best and most confident self? A big part of feeling self-confident is knowing how to prepare for any situation. Write how you would get ready for each of the following:

How would you get ready to take the SATs?

....

....

....

How would you get ready to go on a first date?

....

....

....

How would you get ready to make an important speech?

....

....

....

How would you get ready for a big party where you won't know many people?

....

....

....

Give one or more of these methods a try next time you find yourself needing a self-confidence boost. Which method works best for you?

RELAX:

Being yourself is always the best approach. Take a deep breath and go with the flow.

GET IN A GOOD ROUTINE:

Most often, when you feel good about life, you feel good about yourself. Knowing how to get in your own feel-good routine is a great skill. Is there a song or album that pumps you up, or a certain website you like to read to relax?

KNOW YOURSELF:

Knowing what makes your body and your brain work best is an important way to feel prepared mentally and physically. This means paying attention to sleep and nutrition, and surrounding yourself with good friends in places that make you happy.

TRUST YOURSELF:

Knowing when to say "no" and when to say "yes" is one of the greatest skills a person of any age can master. Trust your gut—don't be afraid to say "no" to a situation that makes you feel unhappy, unsafe, or uncomfortable.

The Art of Saying No

Self-confident people often have strong, healthy boundaries. Knowing when you need time and energy for yourself is an important skill—and one that can be difficult to keep in balance. Sometimes saying no—to doing a favor for a friend or taking on an extra burden at school—can be the best decision you make.

YOU IN A CAPSULE

Merriam-Webster dictionary describes a time capsule as: "a container holding historical records or objects representative of current culture that is deposited for preservation until discovery by some future age."

If you were to make a time capsule of your own, what would you include? Here are some ideas to get you started:

"MY FAVORITE PERFUMES—SMELL MEMORIES ARE SO POWERFUL!" **RACHEL R.**

"MY CHEERLEADING STUFF!" **SUZANNE J.**

"A PICTURE OF MY MOM AND DAD STANDING IN FRONT OF A GIANT MOOSE MADE OUT OF CHOCOLATE." **ANNE K.**

Here's your time capsule: fill it however you like. Draw, color, paste-in the items you would like a "future age" to discover.

"CAN YOU HEAR ME?"

Communication is the single most important part of relating to and working with others. We don't often think about communication—it feels like something that just, well, happens. But when you pay attention to how you communicate—talking, texting, writing a term paper or college admissions essay—you give other people the best chance to understand you.

THE NOT-REALLY-LISTENING

So focused on fighting back or what they'll say next, the Not-Really-Listening person heard nothing of what you were trying to say.

• **If they're not listening to you:** Is there anything you can learn from what the other person is telling you? What's their side of the story? Try to find common ground.

• **If you're not listening to them:** Hearing is different from listening. Make sure you're paying attention to what the other person is saying, and really try to think about how you would feel if you were in that person's shoes.

THE LOST-YOUR-VOICE

When faced with a challenging situation, the Lost-Your-Voice shuts down and shuts up.

• **If they've lost their voice:** All people deserve the space to tell someone if their feelings have been hurt. If you sense something's wrong, ask. Give the other person the chance to speak up. You may not get a response, but letting them know they can be honest and open is your best first step.

• **If you've lost yours:** Dig deep and be honest with yourself about how something made you feel. Be strong and try to find your voice! Expressing your feelings is a critical step in communication.

THE LOST-YOUR-TEMPER

Not a whole lot of fun to talk to, the Lost-Your-Temper gets angry when they're feeling attacked or the conversation isn't going their way.

• **If they've lost their temper:** The result of one person getting mad is that the other person gets mad for the first person being mad at them so the first person gets even madder and . . . you get the idea. Sometimes it's better to wait until everyone's calm before talking about a heated topic.

• **If you're losing your temper:** Keep your temper in check by thinking of how you're presenting your words, and how they might sound to the person you're talking to. You're entitled to feel angry. But how you act on those feelings makes a huge difference.

THE MISUNDERSTANDER

The Misunderstander took something the wrong way, and now no one knows what you're even arguing about anymore.

• **If they've misunderstood:** It can be hard to tell when someone's not quite picking up what you're laying down. If things seems to be going wrong, take a pause and really listen to what the other person is saying before you start trying to correct them.

• **If you've misunderstood:** Many arguments happen because we think people are thinking or doing something they aren't actually thinking or doing. If what someone's saying seems totally off-base, clarify out loud what you think you've heard. Saying it out loud gives them the chance to put things right.

"CAN YOU HEAR ME?"

CONTINUED

"Watch your tone, young lady." The phrase sounds like something your great-grandmother might have said, doesn't it? But it's actually good advice. It's not just *what* you say to other people, but *how* you say it, that can make a huge difference. This activity proves it.

Ready to do some acting? Practice saying the same sentence four different ways, with different emotions behind the words. Listen and hear how different the meanings can be!

"I'll see you soon." (**sad**)
"I'll see you soon." (**caring**)
"I'll see you soon." (**annoyed**)
"I'll see you soon." (**excited**)

Can you come up with your own example sentence and emotions?

"Where have you been?" (**curious**)
"Where have you been?" (**hurt**)
"Where have you been?" (**suspicious**)
"Where have you been?" (**angry**)

"PERHAPS THERE IS A LANGUAGE WHICH IS NOT MADE OF WORDS AND EVERYTHING IN THE WORLD UNDERSTANDS IT. PERHAPS THERE IS A SOUL HIDDEN IN EVERYTHING AND IT CAN ALWAYS SPEAK, WITHOUT EVEN MAKING A SOUND, TO ANOTHER SOUL."

–FRANCES HODGSON BURNETT, *A LITTLE PRINCESS*

WHAT DO YOU BELIEVE?

SOME PEOPLE'S BELIEFS ARE BASED IN A RELIGION. OTHERS' BELIEFS ARE A SET OF MORALS AND VALUES. WHETHER OR NOT YOU'RE RELIGIOUS, YOUR BELIEFS ARE WHAT MOST AFFECT HOW YOU LIVE YOUR LIFE. THE WORLD IS A COMPLICATED PLACE, AND THERE'S NO WAY AROUND THAT. DECISIONS THAT INVOLVE RIGHT AND WRONG HAVE TO BE MADE EVERY DAY—BY YOU, AND BY THE PEOPLE AROUND YOU.

DECIDE WHERE YOU STAND RIGHT NOW ON A SCALE OF 1 TO 5 FOR EACH MAJOR ISSUE BELOW.
AND REMEMBER, FIGURING OUT WHAT YOU BELIEVE IS A LIFELONG JOURNEY. THIS IS ONLY A
STARTING POINT. THE BEST PART ABOUT BEING HUMAN IS YOU CAN ALWAYS CHANGE YOUR MIND!

1 = TOTALLY DISAGREE
5 = TOTALLY AGREE

I go with my gut when deciding what's right and what's wrong.
○ 1　　　　○ 2　　　　○ 3　　　　○ 4　　　　○ 5

I follow religious teachings and customs.
○ 1　　　　○ 2　　　　○ 3　　　　○ 4　　　　○ 5

Government leaders should do what's best for most people.
○ 1　　　　○ 2　　　　○ 3　　　　○ 4　　　　○ 5

People should never lie or steal.
○ 1　　　　○ 2　　　　○ 3　　　　○ 4　　　　○ 5

**It's important to keep an open mind and listen to others' opinions
(even if I don't agree).**
○ 1　　　　○ 2　　　　○ 3　　　　○ 4　　　　○ 5

Being kind to others is the most important thing.
○ 1　　　　○ 2　　　　○ 3　　　　○ 4　　　　○ 5

Protecting the environment is the most important thing.
○ 1　　　　○ 2　　　　○ 3　　　　○ 4　　　　○ 5

Friends should support each other, no matter what.
○ 1　　　　○ 2　　　　○ 3　　　　○ 4　　　　○ 5

I believe in karma—what you put into the universe comes back to you.
○ 1　　　　○ 2　　　　○ 3　　　　○ 4　　　　○ 5

It's important to fight for what you believe in.
○ 1　　　　○ 2　　　　○ 3　　　　○ 4　　　　○ 5

A Letter to Yourself . . .

Use these pages to **write your present self a letter.** It can be about anything—your ambitions, your fears, your feelings, your beliefs. Be honest, and tell yourself exactly what you're thinking, and what's important, right now.

~This~ CHAPTER IS ABOUT YOUR FUTURE

> "THE FUTURE BELONGS TO
> THOSE WHO BELIEVE IN THE
> BEAUTY OF THEIR DREAMS."
>
> —ELEANOR ROOSEVELT

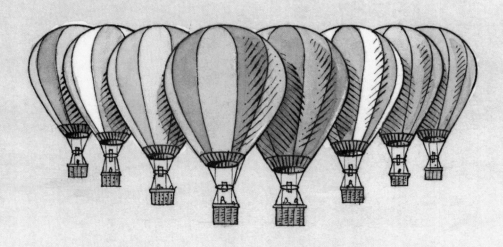

"We do not need magic to change the world.
We carry all the power we need inside ourselves
already: We have the power to imagine better."

J. K. ROWLING

PULL YOURSELF TOGETHER

Looking forward to a bright future? It helps to be organized.
One of the best ways to get organized is to make a list. So let's get started.

. . . .

FILL THIS PAGE WITH ALL THE THINGS YOU NEED
TO DO IN THE NEXT TWO WEEKS.

. . . .

01 _____ ☐

02 _____ ☐

03 _____ ☐

04 _____ ☐

05 _____ ☐

06 _____ ☐

07 _____ ☐

08 _____ ☐

09 _____ ☐

10 _____ ☐

11 _____ ☐

12 _____ ☐

"ORGANIZING IS WHAT YOU DO BEFORE YOU DO SOMETHING, SO THAT WHEN YOU DO IT, IT IS NOT ALL MIXED UP"

–A. A. MILNE, AUTHOR OF *WINNIE-THE-POOH*

FILL THIS PAGE WITH ALL THE THINGS YOU'D LIKE
TO DO IN THE NEXT YEAR.

01 _____ ☐

02 _____ ☐

03 _____ ☐

04 _____ ☐

05 _____ ☐

06 _____ ☐

07 _____ ☐

08 _____ ☐

09 _____ ☐

10 _____ ☐

11 _____ ☐

12 _____ ☐

13 _____ ☐

14 _____ ☐

15 _____ ☐

FILL THIS PAGE WITH ALL THE THINGS YOU'D LIKE
TO DO IN THE NEXT FIVE YEARS.

01 _____ ☐

02 _____ ☐

03 _____ ☐

04 _____ ☐

05 _____ ☐

06 _____ ☐

07 _____ ☐

08 _____ ☐

09 _____ ☐

10 _____ ☐

11 _____ ☐

12 _____ ☐

13 _____ ☐

14 _____ ☐

15 _____ ☐

Your Travel Bug

The world is a big, vibrant place, with a zillion wonderful and diverse experiences to be had—so it makes sense that, at one point or another, lots of us get bitten by the travel bug. Some trips are all about fun and relaxation. Other trips are for excitement and adventure. Still other trips are about learning and experiencing new cultures. What will your next journey be?

Where do you most want to travel?

How long would your trip last?

What do you want to experience there?

What kind of souvenirs would you bring home?

Who would be your traveling companion(s)?

What would you want to gain from your trip?

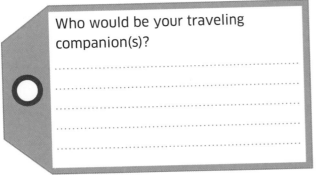

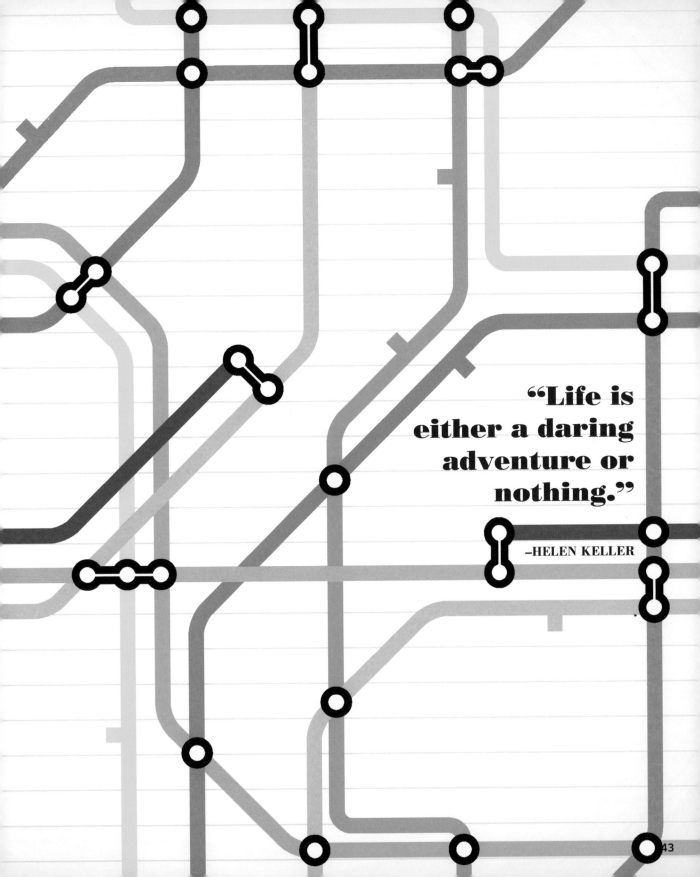

"Life is either a daring adventure or nothing."

–HELEN KELLER

Go for Your GOALS

You've probably seen the hashtag #squadgoals around the internet. It's the sort of thing you'd write under a picture of something amazing you'd love to do with your best friends. Riding an inflatable swan at a pool party, à la Taylor Swift? #squadgoals! A picture of cats sitting around a giant pizza? That's #squadgoals if you're a crazy cat person and/or a pizza fiend.

Turn these pages into a collage of your #squadgoals. Cut pictures out of magazines, print out your favorite memes, and draw, sticker, paint your way to awesome.

Go for Your GOALS

When you're five years old, it's OK to answer "a butterfly"
when someone asks, "What do you want to be when you grow up?"
But now you're older and wiser, and that's not going to cut it.

Right now, you're going to do your future self a favor by starting
to plan for your dream life.

I _____ ON THIS, THE _____ DAY OF _____ ,
      name   month

_____ , DO SOLEMNLY SWEAR THAT IN THE YEAR_____
year   year

I'D LIKE TO BE _____ .

(For example: "the owner of my own candy store," "a scientist
developing a cure for cancer," "mayor of my town," etc.)

AND HERE'S HOW I'M GOING TO GET THERE:

Today I will:

(Research famous women entrepreneurs, astronauts, teachers . . .)

♥

This month I will:

(Focus on my _____.
Or practice my _____.)

♥

This year I will:

(Get better grades in math so I can get into a good engineering school.)

♥

Five years from now I will:

(Dream big!)

♥

YOU LOOKING UP

In ancient Greece, a hero was someone known for bravery or great feats of strength. Heroes were held in the highest esteem and said to be favored by the gods. In modern times, "hero" can mean many things. We asked some of the awesome girls we know to tell us about the heroes they admire the most.

"I admire Marcus Garvey because he was an activist and fought for African-American rights."
–CHLOE C.

"My mother is a strong, independent, persistent woman with a big heart."
–KENIA B.

"You never know why someone's tough on you until there is a mountain that you have to climb alone. Mrs. Joseph, my Spanish teacher, inspires me to keep pushing even when I doubt myself. She's that little bit of faith that can get me through the entire day."
–ASHLENE C.

"Malala Yousafzai. She is a brave, smart, and involved girl."
–RUTHIE G.

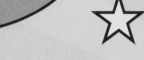

"I admire my parents because they try very hard to give me a good life and everything I want, even when it's hard for them." –SHANIA S.

"Megan Fairchild inspires me. She's a professional dancer who dances in a ballet company and on Broadway." –ELLA T.

"I chose Simone Biles because she has had a difficult life and surpassed all the challenges she has faced to become one of the most successful athletes of all time. Being a gymnast myself, I know how difficult it is to be in the gym and train for competitions. The amount of time Simone had to dedicate to gymnastics to reach the level she is at is inspiring. I know I am not going to be an Olympic gymnast, but watching Simone compete does motivate me to work a little harder."
–SAVANNAH J.

149

MAKING YOUR
BIG DECISIONS

Our days are filled with decisions. Should I get up or hit snooze? Help my brother with the dishes or sit here and send pointless texts to a friend? Fake a cramp and go home or stay after school and make running practice? Just picking up this book and reading it right now was a decision.

But what if you need to make a really big decision like picking a college or taking a new job or running for mayor or choosing to become a mom? How would you handle it?

Some people make snap decisions, going with their instincts. Others agonize over the pros and cons, making lists, charts, and graphs to come up with the absolute best answer possible. There isn't one right way to make big decisions because there are no right decisions. Every choice you make will take your path in a new direction.

We're here to help. Follow these steps, take a breath, and get ready to be an empowered-decision maker!

ASSESS YOURSELF

Think about the last biggish decision you made. What was the decision?

....

....

On a scale of 1-10, how much did the outcome mean to you?

|———————————————————|———————————————————|

1 = "Not much—it didn't really matter."　　　　　　　　5　　　　　　　　10 = "It meant a lot to me. I really wanted to make the absolute best decision."

How much time did you spend thinking about this decision?

....

Did you do any work to help you make the decision? (YouTube searching, talking to friends, writing a list of pros and cons?)

....

Were you anxious about making this decision? Totally confident?

....

Once you made the decision, how confident were you that you made the best possible decision?

....

|———————————————————|———————————————————|

1 = "Not confident at all—I rushed into making the decision."　　　　5　　　　10="I really thought it through and I'm confident I made the best decision with the information I had."

Now look over your answers. When the next big deciding moment comes your way, are you ready? Over the next few pages we'll give you some decision-making tools to help improve your process so you're excited to make informed decisions every single day.

Here's one of the simplest and most effective ways to help you make decisions big and small: a list of pros and cons. (You know: List all the good things about the decision—the pros—then list the bad things—the cons—and see how the decision measures up.)

Use this page to practice getting into the pro-and-con method.

EXAMPLE: If I don't sign up for gymnastics this year	
PRO	**CON**
I'll have more time to study.	I won't get to compete in the state tournament.

NOW IT'S YOUR TURN: What's your big decision? Write it at the top of your list. What are the pros and cons?

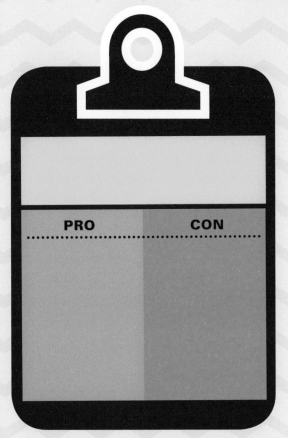
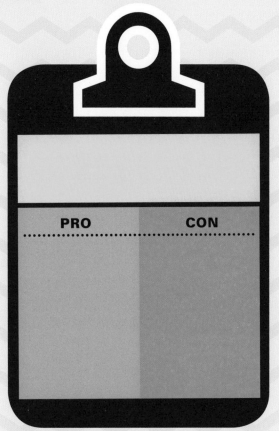

Now look over your lists and use that data to choose the best possible decision. How? Consider these questions:

Is one list longer than the other?

Was it easier to come up with pros or cons?

Did you find yourself rooting for one decision over another while you made your list?

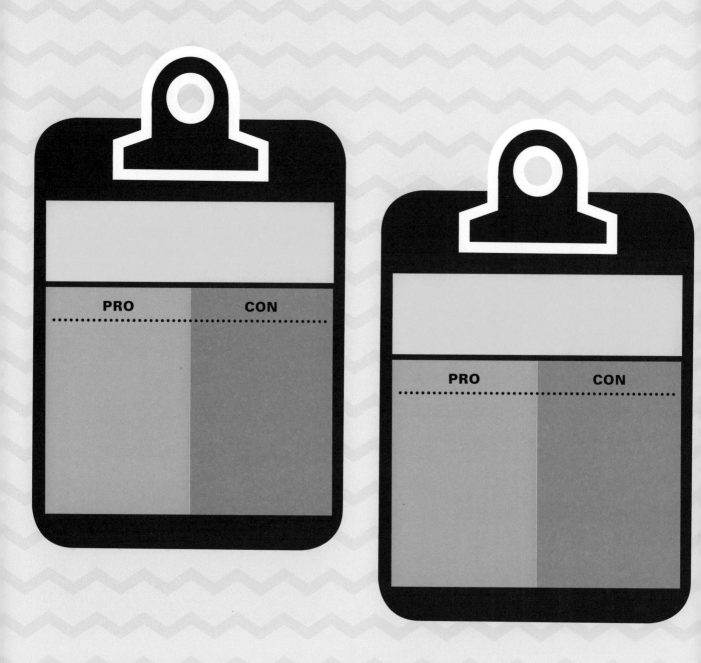

PRO   CON

PRO   CON

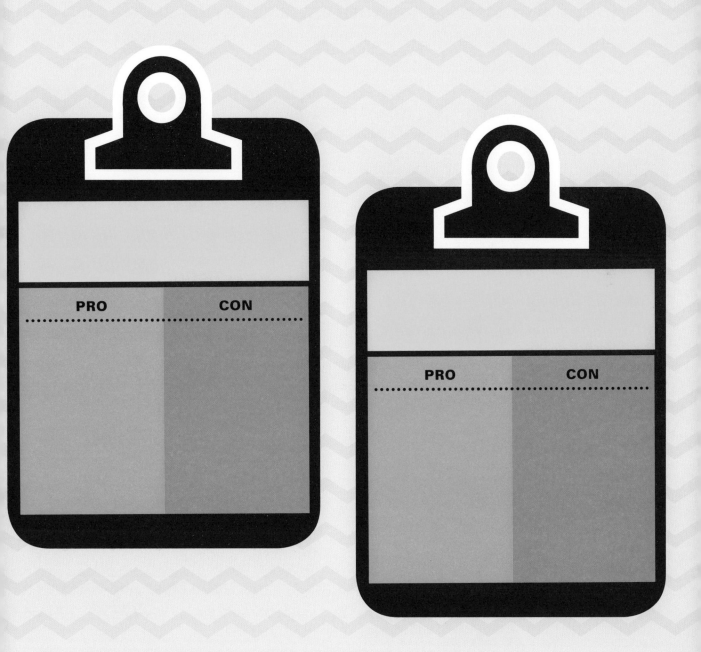

PRO   CON

PRO   CON

BOTTOM LINE: There are pros and cons to just about every decision you have to make. Give yourself the best shot at making a good decision by taking the time to think it through. Trusting your gut helps, too.

MAKING YOUR BIG DECISIONS

CONTINUED

MIND MAPPING IS ANOTHER WAY you can work through a decision. What's mind mapping? It's a visual representation of ideas. You can use it to organize your thoughts, which can be super useful when you're trying to make a big decision.

It's a whole lot easier to show you how this works than to tell you. Here's an example: Say you're trying to decide if you'll take a summer job as a camp counselor. Here's how a mind map of the thought process might help you.

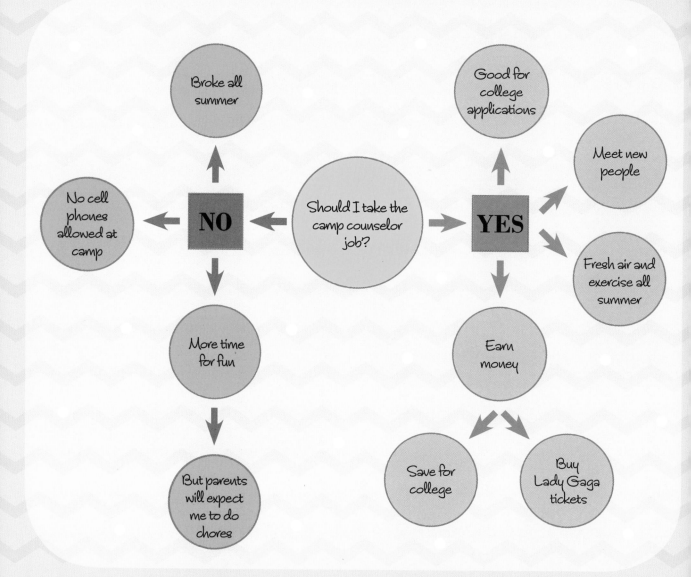

Now create your own mind map about a decision that you have to make.

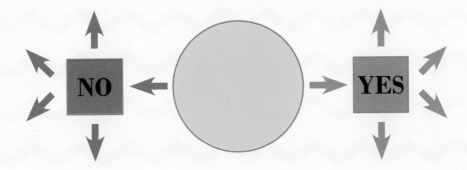

YOU BETTER WORK

WHAT'S YOUR DREAM JOB? DON'T KNOW YET? NO PROBLEM. THE CAREER FAIR'S IN TOWN, AND THESE JOB SECTORS WANT YOU. GRAB A HIGHLIGHTER AND RUN IT OVER ANYTHING ON THESE PAGES THAT SEEMS UP YOUR ALLEY. THEN PUT A HEART

OVER THE JOB SECTORS THAT SEEM PERFECT, A STAR ON THE ONES YOU'D CONSIDER, AND A BIG X THROUGH THE ONES THAT ARE NO-GOS. (BUT BEFORE DRAWING THAT X, ASK YOURSELF: WHY NOT? ARE YOU SURE YOU WOULDN'T GIVE IT A TRY?)

ADMINISTRATION AND BUSINESS MANAGEMENT: Decision-making. Organizational abilities. Problem-solving. Leadership. These are the key aspects of administration and business management. Join this sector and truly excel.

ANIMALS, FARMING, AND THE ENVIRONMENT:

Who doesn't love animals, plants, and working the land? From grooming horses and caring for sick animals to researching crop cultivation, careers in this sector are really *growing*. (Get it?!)

ARTS, CRAFTS, AND DESIGN:

Have artistic talent and an eye for style? Consider a career in arts, crafts, and design! In this sector, you can create new products, style home interiors, or dream up the latest fashions.

ENGINEERING AND MANUFACTURING:

Spend your time analyzing the science behind it all. Join us and learn how things work—and how to make them better. If you're creative, methodical, and organized, you'll thrive here.

CONSTRUCTION:

"Build" your career in the construction sector! We need a steady supply of skilled personnel to keep up with huge demand. If you enjoy practical, hands-on work, there's a job here for you.

FINANCE, LAW, AND POLITICS:

Jobs in this sector require the strongest intellect, the best people skills, the highest numerical abilities, the deepest understanding of legal and business issues. Do you have what it takes?

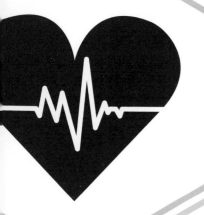

HEALTH AND MEDICINE:

The health-care sector has roles based in hospitals or in the community. With an aptitude for science and technology, and a willingness to work tirelessly for others, you belong in this sector.

INFORMATION TECHNOLOGY AND COMPUTING:

Today's world depends on us, the keepers of high-quality computer networks, websites, and data. Where would the other sectors be without us? Nowhere, that's where.

SALES, MARKETING, AND ADVERTISING:

Commercial flair, an interest in selling, and knowledge of customers are vital here. From creating ads to writing press releases to predicting people's spending habits, this is where it's at.

PERFORMING ARTS, MEDIA, AND JOURNALISM:

Want to perform on stage, play an instrument, write articles, or communicate visually through TV and film? Are you competitive, tenacious, and dedicated? This sector is for you!

SCIENCE AND RESEARCH:

Have an inquiring mind? An analytical approach? The impulse to make new discoveries? In this sector, you could be developing vaccines, discovering marine life, or launching satellites into space. Awesome!

SECURITY AND EMERGENCY SERVICES:

Are you an active person with the drive to help people and society? We want you to join the security and emergency services sector. From army soldiers to firefighters, we get the job done.

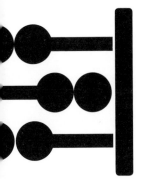

SOCIAL SERVICE AND TEACHING:

Our careers focus on improving people's lives by caring for, training, developing, teaching, and supporting those in need. If you like working with others and have good people skills, you're needed here.

SPORTS, LEISURE, AND TOURISM:

Become a professional athlete, personal trainer, chef, or museum curator in this expanding sector. Enthusiasm for your chosen field, plus a good dose of natural talent, is what it takes.

TRANSPORTATION:

Travel and trade by air, road, rail, and water is increasing. More opportunities are available every day in the transportation sector, in planning roles, and as drivers, pilots, captains, and crew members.

Happy 100th

Happy Birthday! You've lived 100 years, and that's quite an achievement. Spend a little time thinking about the life you've lived, and write the highlights down here. What were your happiest moments? What advice do you have to share with future generations?

Birthday to You!

FAMOUS FOLKS WHO LIVED TO

100

GEORGE BURNS, (1896-1996), comedian and actor

OLIVIA DE HAVILLAND (born in 1916), British-American actress from the Golden Age of Hollywood

DORRIT HOFFLEIT (1907-2007), researcher, astronomer, and mentor to generations of women astronomers

CLAUDE LEVI-STRAUSS (1908-2009), famous French anthropologist

YOUR HERO
HALL of FAME

There's the Baseball Hall of Fame, the Rock & Roll Hall of Fame, the National Toy Hall of Fame, and even a Cockroach Hall of Fame (in Plano, Texas, in case you'd like to visit).

Now it's time to make The _____'s Hero Hall of
(INSERT YOUR NAME HERE)
Fame. In each of the frames here, draw, paste, staple, or tape a picture of your inductees. They should be the people you believe are true heroes in the world, the ones who inspire you to become a future hero yourself. Give a brief explanation under each picture about why you chose them.

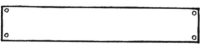

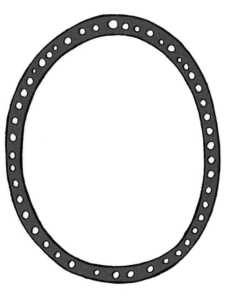

MONEY
ON YOUR MIND

What's your attitude toward money? Your answers to the questions on this quiz will reveal your priorities when it comes to saving and spending.

A FRIEND OF YOURS WINS THE LOTTERY. YOU TELL THEM THEY SHOULD:

- ❏ **A.** Start their own business or website.
- ❏ **B.** Invest the money and save for the future.
- ❏ **C.** Travel the world to see faraway places.
- ❏ **D.** Donate the money to a good cause.

YOU'RE SAVING UP TO BUY A CAR. YOU:

- ❏ **A.** Put your money into a high-interest account to get the biggest yield.
- ❏ **B.** Save a little each month over a long period until you have enough.
- ❏ **C.** Do everything you can to save it quickly so you can have freedom.
- ❏ **D.** Save a little, but don't think about it too much. You can live without.

IT'S THE SUMMER AFTER YOUR HIGH SCHOOL GRADUATION. YOU:

- ❏ **A.** Take summer courses to get a jump on college or learn a new skill.
- ❏ **B.** Focus on getting together the things you need for college.
- ❏ **C.** Road trip with your friends or go to concerts, movies, or other fun events.
- ❏ **D.** Spend the summer expressing yourself through making or building things.

YOU WANT TO GET INVOLVED AND VOLUNTEER, SO YOU DECIDE TO:

- ❏ **A.** Teach unemployed adults how to use computers.
- ❏ **B.** Help out at a soup kitchen.
- ❏ **C.** Travel and build homes with Habitat for Humanity.
- ❏ **D.** Organize an arts festival for underprivileged kids.

YOU'RE VISITING AN ELDERLY RELATIVE. YOU:

- ❏ **A.** Talk to them about their career and ask for financial advice.
- ❏ **B.** See if there's anything they need done around the house.
- ❏ **C.** Talk to them about their adventures and travels.
- ❏ **D.** Take photographs or a video of them for an art project.

YOUR YOUNGER COUSIN ASKS YOU FOR LIFE ADVICE. YOU TELL THEM TO:

- ❏ **A.** Work as hard as they can and always strive for success.
- ❏ **B.** Focus on the basics, like doing well at school and being a good person.
- ❏ **C.** Always try new things and seek out new adventures and experiences.
- ❏ **D.** Follow their heart and live in the moment.

MONEY ON YOUR MIND

MOSTLY As: AMBITIOUS

When you've got a goal in mind, you won't rest until you reach it, and doing so gives you a great sense of accomplishment.

PROS: You've got your finances under control. You know how important it is to save, and you've got the self-control to do it. Watch out, Wall Street! You've got the sense (and cents!) to make it to the top.

CONS: You're so focused on your goals, you may miss out on intriguing detours that come up out of the blue. Make sure you don't let money come between you and relationships. Keep a healthy balance between making money and making time for the people you care about.

MOSTLY Bs: PRACTICAL

Money isn't the first thing on your mind, and when you spend it, you do so practically. You only save for the things that you need. As long as you've got enough funds to live, you're happy.

PROS: You've got your priorities in order. You don't let money consume you, and you know how to save money for something really important.

CONS: Big expenses and opportunities may come up from time to time, and they could seem intimidating when you're used to spending only in small amounts. Remember that it's OK to reward yourself from time to time, when and if you can.

MOSTLY Cs: ADVENTUROUS

For you, money is just a means to having new experiences and adventures. It's not about the money itself, it's about what you can do with it. You're not always the best at saving; you find it hard to say no to the exciting opportunities that pop up day to day.

PROS: You'll never be bored! Lots of exciting opportunities await you, and you want to (and know how to) take advantage of them.

CONS: Saying yes to every exciting opportunity that comes your way means you may find yourself running out of funds fast. And you might want to stay away from credit cards; the temptation to overspend is a tricky one to overcome!

MOSTLY Ds: CREATIVE

Having money means being able to help others, and you find creative ways to use money to make the world a better place. Whether that's actually donating money to charities, or by making art or something others can enjoy, you think of money as an aid to self-expression.

PROS: Giving money to others is noble and makes you feel warm and fuzzy. You're doing the world some good. Money isn't the focus of your life, and you're set for a happier, more fulfilling life because of it.

CONS: You're not the most practical when it comes to spending money on the things you need. Take extra care to make sure you're keeping your eye on the ball when it comes to necessary expenses. Don't be afraid to spend money on yourself when you need to.

YOUR CRYSTAL BALL

Wouldn't it be great if you could look into a crystal ball and see the future? All that planning, studying, deciding, worrying—all of it gone in a glance, because you already know what's coming.

Unfortunately, this isn't a crystal ball you're holding. It's a book. Sorry.

In an effort to be that crystal ball so many of us want, here are two fun games you can play to predict your future. (Just don't take them too seriously—results not guaranteed!)

1. PLAY THE CLASSIC: MASH (MANSION / APARTMENT / SHACK / HOUSE)

This one's for you and a friend. Grab a piece of paper and write the letters "M A S H" at the top. Then choose at least four categories—careers, transportation, types of pets, how many kids you'll have, potential people to marry, places to live, you get the idea—and write them down. Have your friend give you two options for each category, then add two of your own.

HERE'S AN EXAMPLE:

NUMBER OF KIDS YOU'LL HAVE	NAME OF PERSON YOU'LL MARRY	WHICH PET YOU'LL OWN	HOW YOU'LL GET AROUND
0	Joey	dog	turquoise minivan
1	Tyler	cat	motorcycle
3	Carlos	mongoose	school bus
17	Justin Bieber	antelope	llama named Carl

Now, have your friend pick a number from 1 to 12. Starting with the "M" in MASH, count each option until you hit your friend's number—then cross that option off. Keep going, skipping over crossed-off options, until you have one answer left in each category. Then read your friend's future: "You'll live in a mansion with 17 kids, a husband named Joey, and a pet dog, and you'll drive around in a turquoise minivan. Good luck!"

2. FOLD A FORTUNE-TELLER

There's a really good chance you've made a thousand of these. But just in case you've been too busy with, you know, real life, here's how to use a classic fortune-teller.

1. PICK A COLOR FROM THE OUTSIDE OF THE FORTUNE-TELLER, FOR INSTANCE, "RED"—THREE LETTERS.

2. OPEN THE FORTUNE-TELLER ONCE FOR EACH LETTER—SIDEWAYS, UP AND DOWN, SIDEWAYS AGAIN.

3. PICK A NUMBER. OPEN THE FORTUNE-TELLER THAT MANY TIMES.

4. CHOOSE ANOTHER NUMBER AND OPEN THE FLAP TO REVEAL YOUR FORTUNE!

BONUS GAME

Find the answer in a book. Think of a burning question you have, then grab the closest book and close your eyes. Flip to a random page, point somewhere on it, and open your eyes. Read the sentence you're pointing to—there's your answer! It's silly, but give it a try. You could be surprised by how right it ends up being—or at least have a laugh about how wrong it is!

GO WITH YOUR GUT:

TIRED OF ALL THE THINKING THIS BOOK IS MAKING YOU DO? IT'S TIME TO GO WITH YOUR GUT. CIRCLE YOUR ANSWERS BELOW: **WOULD YOU RATHER . . .**

LIVE ON A **TROPICAL ISLAND**

OR

LIVE IN A **BUSTLING CITY?**

INVENT A NEW **MAJOR-LEAGUE SPORT** OR INVENT A NEW KIND OF **COMPUTER?**

BE A FAMOUS **ACTRESS**

OR

BE A FAMOUS **AUTHOR?**

GO ON A **RELAXING VACATION**

OR

GO BACKPACKING THROUGH THE MOUNTAINS?

SET SPECIFIC GOALS AND WORK TOWARD THEM

OR

FIGURE IT OUT **AS YOU GO ALONG?**

GO TO A **SMALL COLLEGE** OR GO TO A **BIG UNIVERSITY?**

BE ABLE TO SEE INTO THE FUTURE OR **BE SURPRISED** BY WHAT HAPPENS?

FUTURE

MEET **YOUR HERO** **OR** BE **SOMEBODY'S HERO?**

WIN AN **OLYMPIC GOLD MEDAL** **OR** WIN THE **NOBEL PRIZE?**

OWN A **BOAT** **OR** OWN A **PLANE?**

MAKE YOUR **OWN DECISIONS** **OR** HAVE SOMEONE SMART **MAKE DECISIONS FOR YOU?**

THROW YOURSELF A **BIRTHDAY PARTY** **OR** HAVE YOUR FRIENDS THROW YOU A **SURPRISE PARTY?**

BECOME PRESIDENT OF **THE UNITED STATES** **OR** PRESIDENT OF A **MAJOR MOVIE STUDIO?**

GO **SKYDIVING** **OR** GO **ROCK CLIMBING?**

BECOME A **VEGETARIAN** **OR** STOP EATING **DAIRY?**

FALL IN **LOVE** **OR** **TRAVEL** THE WORLD?

RIDE A **HOVERBOARD** **OR** DRIVE A **HOVERCAR?**

WHO YOU REALLY ARE

A huge part of growing up is figuring out who you are and what you like. Embarking on new adventures, trying on different hats to match your evolving personality, and making new decisions about who you want to be are all part of how you move from one stage to the next. At this time in your life, you have the wisdom of childhood behind you, and more flexibility than you might have as an adult. It's the perfect time to get to work.

The more insight you have into the way you think and act, the more easily you can work toward your goals and dreams. Use the following tools to learn about yourself, then use that knowledge to help build your future!

FIRST, LET'S TRY SOME WORD ASSOCIATION. READ THE FOLLOWING WORDS
AND WRITE DOWN THE THINGS THAT POP INTO YOUR HEAD. DON'T WORRY
IF THEY SEEM SILLY—JUST TRUST YOURSELF, AND LET IT FLOW . . .

CHANGE

GROWTH

INSPIRATION

MOTIVATION

DEVELOPMENT

MISTAKES

READ OVER YOUR ANSWERS. WHAT CAN YOU LEARN ABOUT YOUR
PERSONALITY FROM THE THINGS YOU WROTE? DO YOU SEE ANY PATTERNS?
ARE THERE ANY SURPRISES?

Next, let's check out your thinking patterns. Learning the different types of thinking patterns can help you figure out where you need help, and where you feel your best! Sometimes thinking about thinking is the best kind of thinking we can do.

Of the seven thinking patterns below, circle the ones that you recognize most in yourself.

Problem-solving: Coming up with solutions; weighing their feasibility; gathering resources; inspiring others to join in; putting a plan into action

Creative thinking: Thinking outside the box; thinking about something in a new and different way; being bold as you come up with and put forth new ideas

Emotional thinking: Using thoughts and feelings to go "behind the scenes" of a situation; figuring out how a person really feels; trying to create a bridge or path to move forward

Impulsive thinking: Going with the flow; seizing the moment; always being ready to act; sometimes getting into trouble by not thinking through the consequences

Decision-making and leadership: Being the one to figure out how to make something happen; planning, organizing, taking control, and putting ideas into motion

Reclusive thinking: Working alone or in small groups; presenting your thoughts to others only after you have had a chance to think carefully on your own

Analytical thinking: Looking at all the pieces of the whole problem to find the answer; working to best understand the question and all its parts

OBVIOUSLY EVERYONE HAS STRENGTHS AND WEAKNESSES. BUT NOT EVERYONE KNOWS THE SECRET TO OVERCOMING THOSE WEAKNESSES: MATCHING THEM WITH YOUR STRENGTHS. FILL OUT THE LISTS BELOW TO DEVELOP YOUR OWN PERSONAL ROAD MAP TO OVERCOMING YOUR WEAKNESSES.

What do you believe are your five greatest strengths and talents?

1...
2...
3...
4...
5...

What are five things that tend to be the most difficult for you?

1...
2...
3...
4...
5...

NOW MATCH EACH WEAKNESS YOU LISTED WITH A STRENGTH. CAN YOU BRAINSTORM IDEAS FOR WAYS TO OVERCOME THE WEAKNESSES USING THE STRENGTH IT'S MATCHED WITH?

WHEN YOU LOOK AHEAD TO YOUR FUTURE, WHAT DO YOU THINK WILL BE THE MOST DIFFICULT CHALLENGES? USING WHAT YOU'VE LEARNED ON THE LAST FOUR PAGES, HOW COULD YOU START TO PREPARE FOR THEM NOW?

WHAT'S YOUR LOVE ATTITUDE?

Some people have a new crush every day. Some people have liked the same person for years. Still others don't really think or care much about romance. How is it that we're all so different? The answer lies in our attitudes about love. Give this quiz a try, then turn the page to learn what your answers reveal about your love attitude.

WHICH OF THESE SOUNDS MOST LIKE YOU?

WHEN I MEET SOMEONE I THINK IS CUTE, THE FIRST THING I TRY TO FIGURE OUT IS:

❏ **A.** Whether they'll be interested in me, and reasons they might not be.

❏ **B.** Whether they seem like they'd be up for a fun date or to go to a party.

❏ **C.** Whether our personalities will match and we'll get along with each other.

WHEN I'M WITH SOMEONE I HAVE A CRUSH ON, I WATCH OUT FOR:

❏ **A.** Signs that I might be doing something wrong, or something that will put them off.

❏ **B.** Signs that they're way too into me, when I'm just having fun crushing.

❏ **C.** Signs that they'll treat me well if we ended up in a relationship.

IF I'M KEEPING MY CRUSH A SECRET FROM THEM, IT'S PROBABLY BECAUSE I:

❏ **A.** Am afraid that they won't feel the same way about me.

❏ **B.** Am just enjoying the crush and don't want things to get dramatic.

❏ **C.** Am hoping they feel the same way and will make the first move.

IF I'M NOT IN A RELATIONSHIP, I'LL PROBABLY:

❏ **A.** Worry I'll be alone forever, and maybe date someone just to reassure myself.

❏ **B.** Enjoy the freedom and have fun with my friends or flirting with my crushes.

❏ **C.** Just enjoy life, and wait for someone I really like to come along.

IF I EVER GOT IN AN ARGUMENT WITH A FUTURE BOYFRIEND OR GIRLFRIEND, I'D PROBABLY:

❏ **A.** Worry that they'd break up with me because of it.

❏ **B.** End the relationship before things got really intense.

❏ **C.** Try to work it out, but accept whatever happened.

WHAT'S YOUR **LOVE** ATTITUDE?

CONTINUED

WHAT COULD YOUR ANSWERS SHOW ABOUT YOUR ATTITUDE WHEN IT COMES TO LOVE?

Mostly **A**s:

Is your love attitude **anxious**? People who are anxious about love may assume they're not good enough for the person they like. They're so eager to be in love, they tend to overlook the other person's flaws, assuming anything wrong in the relationship is their own fault. Anxious people may fall in love quickly—which isn't always a bad thing. But it can be if the match really isn't right. If this sounds like you, make sure you have a real connection with someone—one that includes trust and mutual respect, not just one that gives you butterflies—to avoid mistaking an exciting crush for love.

Mostly **B**s:

Do you try to **avoid** love? People who are avoidant are often scared of getting hurt, so they keep their crushes at a distance. This doesn't mean they're not romantic; actually, many dream of finding "the one," that perfect match. It's not unusual, either, for avoidants to stay in love with an ex, longing for a lost love instead of looking ahead. If this sounds like you, remember: Real love can take time (and yes, sometimes it can hurt). But don't be so quick to end a good thing. Be open to love if it shows up.

Mostly **C**s:

Is your love attitude **attached**? People with this attitude have a good grip on what goes into true love: passion (those butterflies you feel), closeness (that feeling of connection with another person), and commitment (being willing to put in the effort). They might have anxious or avoidant feelings, too, but they keep them in check. Being in love is no easy task. The best way you can help yourself is to always be clear, to yourself and others, about what you want and what you need from any relationship.

"BEING DEEPLY LOVED BY SOMEONE GIVES YOU **STRENGTH,** WHILE LOVING SOMEONE DEEPLY GIVES YOU **COURAGE."**
—LAO TZU

You Got This

Sometimes difficult things happen to us or around us—things we have no control over. You may feel helpless in the face of a personal disaster, angry at a decision someone else made, or scared of or saddened by something that happened in the world. Fortunately, when these challenges crash into your path, you have a unique opportunity: Each challenge can make you more aware of your own special strengths. With the right attitude and tools, you can prepare yourself to deal with future obstacles.

{ On this page, list some major events you felt like you had no control over. They can be things that happened to you personally or things that happened in the world. Write how each event made you feel. When you've finished, turn the page to learn more. }

What happened:

I felt _____ because: ....
....
....

What happened:

I felt _____ because: ....
....
....

What happened:

I felt _____ because: ....
....
....

What happened:

I felt _____ because: ....
....
....

The difficult things that happen to you hold big opportunities for learning about yourself, and for gaining the strength and maturity you need to deal with future situations. The ways in which you learn to cope with these challenges could end up being some of the most important parts of your personality. The ability to get through tough times is something you'll need your entire life.

FOR EACH OF THE EVENTS YOU LISTED ON THE PREVIOUS PAGE, THINK ABOUT THE FOLLOWING QUESTIONS:

1. Which tool (or tools) most helped you through each event: acceptance, forgiveness, gratitude, compassion, or spirituality? Or was there something or somebody else that gave you comfort?

2. Did any good things come from each event, even if it seemed like it was entirely bad at the time?

3. Did going through those challenges change how you see the world, or how you see yourself?

4. If someone you cared about was about to go through the same event, what advice would you give him or her?

{ Working on how you handle tough situations is key, but it's just as important to make sure you've got the right people around to help you through the most difficult times. Talking to and leaning on a friend, sibling, parent, teacher, or someone else you trust are some of the best ways you can prepare yourself for stumbling blocks. }

Who are the four people you trust the most and can lean on when the going gets tough? Why?

I trust _____

because

I trust _____

because

I trust _____

because

I trust _____

because

BUILDING YOUR FUTURE

Dear Reader,

SURPRISE! IT'S NOT TODAY. IT'S 20 YEARS FROM TODAY, 20____.
(ARE THERE FLYING CARS? WE HOPE THERE ARE FLYING CARS.)
SPEND SOME TIME HERE THINKING ABOUT THE LIFE YOU'D LIKE TO BE LIVING
WHEN YOU'RE (YOUR AGE + 20) YEARS OLD: _____.

Where do you live?

What's your job? What do you do every day?

How do you spend your free time?

Who greets you when you get home from work?

Are you happy? Fulfilled? Challenged? Anxious?

Dear Reader,

YOU'RE BACK IN PRESENT TIME. HELLO, AGAIN!
NOW IT'S TIME TO DO THE SERIOUS WORK OF GETTING BACK TO THE FUTURE YOU JUST IMAGINED. WHAT STEPS DO YOU NEED TO TAKE NOW TO GET YOURSELF WHERE YOU WANT TO BE IN THE YEAR 20___?

What do you need to do TODAY?

What do you need to do NEXT MONTH?

What do you need to do NEXT YEAR?

Your Changing World

In the previous activity, you predicted what your life would be like in 20 years. It's time to put on your fortune-teller hat again. (Metaphorically speaking, of course. Unless you actually have a fortune-teller hat, in which case, you do you.) This time let's focus on the world around you. How do you think it will change in the next 20 years?

FOR EACH CATEGORY, WRITE OR DRAW YOUR PREDICTIONS.

TECHNOLOGY

TRAVEL

HEALTH

ENVIRONMENT

ENTERTAINMENT

SCHOOL

Hello, Future You . . .

Use these pages to write a letter to yourself **10 years from now**. What do you hope Future You is doing? Where do you live? Who do you love? What is most important for you to remember?

"It is important for all of us to appreciate where we come from and how that history has really shaped us in ways that we might not understand."

–SONIA SOTOMAYOR,
Associate Justice of the United States Supreme Court

PHOTO CREDITS

The publisher would like to thank the following for their kind permission to reproduce their photographs:

(Key: a-above; b-below/bottom; c-center; f-far; l-left; r-right; t-top)

6 **123RF.com:** Liliia Rudchenko / rudchenko. 7 **123RF.com:** Liliia Rudchenko / rudchenko. 43 **Getty Images:** C Squared Studios / Photodisc. 90 **123RF.com:** Boris Stromar / astrobobo (c). 93 **123RF.com:** Boris Stromar / astrobobo (tr). 116-119 **123RF.com:** Liliia Rudchenko / rudchenko. 124 **123RF.com:** Anastasia Popova / bersonne. 126 **123RF. com:** Teguh Mujiono / tigatelu. 143 **123RF.com:** tovovan. 166-167 **123RF.com:** Vladimir Yudin / rrraven

All other images © Dorling Kindersley

For further information see: www.dkimages.com

FROM RACHEL
I'd like to thank: Our editor, Nancy Ellwood, and designer, Jessica Lee. The Kempster Clan. The awesome students of Tammy O'Donnell and Laina Joseph. And always, Matthew Barry. Best. Husband. Ever.

FROM JOANNAH
I would like to thank my husband Keyvan, my family, and my friends for their support and encouragement, and the wonderful editors at DK for their brilliance, affability, and determination in making this book into reality.

FROM ALLIE
My thanks go out to the many awe-inspiring people I've been lucky enough to work with throughout my life—not the least of which include Nancy Ellwood and Jessica Lee. And to three amazing Singers—Judy, Hartley, and Lauren—who I know always have my back. Love you.

FROM JESSICA
I'd like to thank everyone who helped me make this book, and give a special shout-out to Peter and Drew for their love and support.

191